YOUR GROWING
RELATIONSHIP WITH JESUS

Living the
STORY

GENERAL EDITOR
DAN WOLGEMUTH
Along with the 3Story® Team

YOUTH FOR CHRIST USA

CROSSWAY BOOKS
WHEATON, ILLINOIS

Library of Congress Cataloging-in-Publication Data
Living the story : your growing relationship with Jesus / Dan Wolgemuth, editor.
    p. cm.
  ISBN 978-1-58134-955-9 (tpb)
  1. Spiritual formation. I. Wolgemuth, Daniel S. II. Title.
BV4511.L585   2007
248.4—dc22   2007009118

ML		17	16	15	14	13	12	11	10	09	08	07
15	14	13	12	11	10	9	8	7	6	5	4	3	2	1

Living the Story is dedicated to the volunteers and student leaders of Youth for Christ.

Your devotion to Jesus and deep commitment to love and share the Good News with teenagers who are not yet living the story is the heartbeat of this book.

We are honored to serve with you.

Contents

Contributing Authors

Jenny Morgan, YFC/USA, Denver

Trent Bushnell, Lansing, MI YFC

Jack Crabtree, Long Island, NY YFC

Nina Edwards, YFC/USA, Denver

Byron Emmert, YFC/USA, Denver

Teddi Pettee, Sacramento, CA YFC

Tara Posen, Southern California YFC

Welcome!

Your relationship with Jesus is a thrilling adventure. *Living the Story* was created to help you experience life with Christ in a way that helps you know Him in a powerful and more personal way.

Throughout the ages people have attempted to know about the story of God, to understand and participate in God's divine architecture. We believe that's exactly what He wants for all of us—a real experience with the One True God, an authentic encounter with the Living God through His one and only Son, Jesus Christ. He wrote our stories long ago, hoping that we'd want to live the story with Him. He invites each of us and any of us to follow His plan for our lives by placing our trust in Christ alone. He gives us the gifts of His grace, mercy, and love. He pursues us like a great storyteller pursues the greatest story.

The most important story ever told is God's Story. God is both the author and participant in this incredible story.

He included us in His story. God made room for you and me in His story. *Living the Story* is an invitation to learn more about this beautiful, unfolding story with God.

So, Where Do We Begin?

Living the Story begins by acknowledging that questions often guide the way when we explore God's Story. God is neither afraid nor intimidated by our questions and doubts. In fact, He uses our curiosities, misgivings, and uncertainties to strengthen our faith in Him.

The first question to consider is this: *do you remember when you began to intentionally engage in God's Story?* Remembering how it all began for you will provide the foundation to your story. This foundation can strengthen your ongoing understanding of God's Story.

Perhaps you aren't quite sure when you first encountered Jesus. Maybe the moment you met God is a little blurry. It is possible that you haven't yet begun your relationship with Jesus, but you're interested, and you're looking for some answers to questions about God. Wherever you find yourself in God's emerging story, *Living the Story* might help.

Try this: do you remember when you started to be interested in Jesus Christ? Write a date or location down that reminds you of this important encounter.

....

....

....

....

It's okay to be unsure, to ask questions. It's even okay to admit that this might be the very first step in that process. In the space below, write down a phrase or two that describes the beginning of your story with Jesus, even if it's a question.

....

....

....

....

Part of God's Story teaches us that we can be sure about our relationship with Him. Our prayer is that *Living the Story* will help you live with more confidence and certainty about Jesus and His love for you and the way that He includes you in His story.

What Part Does the Bible Play?

Why do we use the Bible in our discussions about *Living the Story*? Because we have discovered the Bible to be full of wisdom for anyone who takes the time to connect with God through His written Word (the Bible.) Most of the Bible passages used in *Living the Story* are printed for you, so you don't have to worry about knowing how to find things (though finding specific Bible stories and passages is a great skill to learn and will help you along the way).

We especially tried to encounter Jesus Christ and the many ways He taught, loved, listened, and lived His life on Planet Earth. He was also a master storyteller. We think His life, death, and resurrection are the keys to understanding how to live your story with God and with each other.

Bible passages are usually printed in the English Standard Version (ESV), a current, accurate, trustworthy translation of the Bible. At times we used additional translations like the New International Version (NIV) or the New Living Translation (NLT) as well as two paraphrases of the Bible, The Message (TM) and The Living Bible (TLB). These enable us to understand especially difficult concepts in the Bible.

What Is the Format of Each Chapter?

Living the Story is put together in seven sections within each of the seven chapters.

1. **INTRODUCTIONS**—Questions and activities to draw us into a topic
2. **GOD'S STORY**—Exploration of a specific story from Jesus' life, straight out of the Bible
3. **INVESTIGATE THE STORY**—Questions to ask God and guided experiences with God's Story
4. **DISCOVER MORE OF THE STORY**—Help from additional passages of the Bible
5. **MY STORY**—Real-life, true stories
6. **OUR STORY**—Examination of the importance of community and what it means to be part of a group of Christ followers. This will also contain questions to ask your friends who are following Jesus and activities to try out with them
7. **THE STORY CONTINUES**—Specific challenges to keep you going with God and questions to ask your friends who are not yet following Jesus

How Do We Use Living the Story?

If you are by yourself reading and working on *Living the Story,* a few simple guidelines will assist you in having a great experience with God. Consider these.

>> Be open to the spiritual growth with Jesus that will happen when you read.

>> Try your best to find answers in the Bible as *Living the Story* guides you along.

>> Ask questions—first of God, then of other followers of Christ you know.

>> Listen carefully to God.

>> Have fun!

>> Give yourself the freedom to skip things if you're too confused.

>> Share your developing story with someone you love and trust.

If you are facilitating a group of people using *Living the Story,* consider carefully your role. God probably wants to use you as a guide, not a lecturer. So, listen well—to Him and to the people in your group. Look for the natural story connections between your group participants and God as well as between each of their stories and your own story.

Living the Story ends with some helpful tools and insights to assist you in continuing to grow with God. Web sites, summaries, and ways to celebrate your relationship with Jesus all allow you to discover how to stay connected to God after you finish this book.

It is an honor and a joy to live the story with you through this book! You're not alone.

Dan Wolgemuth
General Editor

{ CHAPTER 1

What Do I Need to Know?
UNDERSTANDING MY RELATIONSHIP WITH GOD

Questions, Questions, Questions, Questions

Like most new Christians, you probably have lots of questions about what's next in your life with Jesus. You may have wondered, for example . . .

>> What does it really mean that Jesus is now living in me?
>> Will I really go to heaven someday?
>> Could God change the deal on me?
>> What if this Good News about Jesus being my Savior doesn't last?

Or you may have harbored some doubts.

>> Write down the first three questions that come to your mind when you think about your new relationship with Jesus.

....

....

....

Questions are good! One of the greatest privileges of your personal relationship with the God of the universe is that you can ask Him any question. He wants you to bring it on because He loves you and desires for you to know Him. This book is designed to help you learn more about connecting God's Story to your story as you take the next steps in following Jesus.

Take one minute right now to talk to God.

>> Thank Him for having more answers than you have questions.
>> Thank Him for loving you so much that He sent Jesus to die on the cross for you.

>> Now tell Him anything else that's on your mind—He's listening.

Use your imagination.

What if another student in your school or neighborhood were suddenly killed in an accident? He was a great guy who was liked by almost everyone.

Your community is in shock, and a ton of people come to his funeral. You and about twenty of his closest friends are hanging out at your house a couple of days later. It's tough. The grief is heavy. Lots of stories and tears are tied together with the pain of knowing that your lives just won't be the same without your friend.

Suddenly another person is standing in the middle of your group! The doors are shut and haven't been opened, so you're sort of taken back by the presence of another person next to you. Within seconds everyone knows what they think they're seeing, but no one can believe their eyes—*it's your friend who died, but now he is looking very much alive!*

Okay, time-out! Play the part of a scriptwriter here, and write down the first five comments that you hear from your friends and yourself.

>> The first words out of your mouth: ....
....

>> Then the first words your friends might say: ....
....

>> Then you might reply: ....
....

>> Then your friends might say: ....
....

>> Then you would say: ....
....

Do you agree or disagree with any of this? Once your group realizes that your friend has risen from the dead, you will pay close attention to everything he says and will want to know how and why he came back from death.

God's Story

As you read this part of God's Story in Luke 24:36-48 . . .

>> know that it is Sunday evening, two days after Jesus died on the cross, and Jesus' close friends are in an upstairs room of a home.

>> know that these friends are grieving and talking about their Lord's suffering and death.

>> know that two other followers of Jesus had just rushed into the room with *big news:* they had seen Jesus very much alive.

>> look for the reason why this eyewitness account by Luke is so important to your new faith in Jesus.

>> imagine the emotions and thoughts running wild in the minds of Jesus' followers. Put yourself in the middle of this incredible scene!

[36]As they were talking about these things, Jesus himself stood among them, and said to them, "Peace to you!" [37]But they were startled and frightened and thought they saw a spirit. [38]And he said to them, "Why are you troubled, and why do doubts arise in your hearts? [39]See my hands and my feet, that it is I myself. Touch me, and see. For a spirit does not have flesh and bones as you see that I have." [40]And when he had said this, he showed them his hands and his feet. [41]And while they still disbelieved for joy and were marveling, he said to them, "Have you anything here to eat?" [42]They gave him a piece of broiled fish, [43]and he took it and ate before them.

[44]Then he said to them, "These are my words that I spoke to you while I was still with you, that everything written about me in the Law of Moses and the Prophets and the Psalms must be fulfilled." [45]Then he opened their minds to understand the Scriptures, [46]and said to them, "Thus it is written, that the Christ should suffer and on the third day rise from the dead, [47]and that repentance and forgiveness of sins should be proclaimed in his name to all nations, beginning from Jerusalem. [48]You are witnesses of these things."

Investigate the Story

>> Why do you think Jesus wanted His followers in the upper room to look at His hands and feet and touch Him?

....

....

....

>> Jesus pointed out to His friends that He had fulfilled the prophecy of His death and resurrection. Why was it was so important for His followers to understand these events?

....

....

....

Don't miss this: If Jesus Christ had not risen from the dead, you would not be reading this book. This book and the Bible would have no reason to exist! Jesus would have been nothing more than a nice spiritual teacher without the power to be the Savior for the world. We would be hopelessly condemned for our sins.

Jesus came to earth as both God and human and lived a perfect life. He said His death on the cross would pay the penalty for our sins. Because of Him, we can be forgiven. He gives us a relationship with God and life in heaven for eternity. But what if His body were still in the tomb? End of story. Jesus' resurrection proves that everything He ever taught and promised is true. Jesus is the only Savior! One of His disciples, Peter, said it this way: *That's what Christ did definitively: suffered because of others' sins, the Righteous One for the unrighteous ones. He went through it all—was put to death and then made alive—to bring us to God* (1 Peter 3:18, *The Message*).

Discover More of the Story

Let's back up in God's Story for a moment. Christ's resurrection proved that He is the *Lord* of all! Why does God's Story refer to Jesus as "Savior and Lord"? It's because of what He accomplished on the cross for us.

>> How many crosses have you seen in the last week in pictures, jewelry, etc.?

....

>> How many of the people you see wearing a cross are actually followers of Jesus?

....

>> How would your belief in God's Story be different without Christ's cross?

....

God's Word teaches us what Christ's *cross* means for every follower of Jesus.

CHRIST'S CROSS . . .

Communicates God's unconditional love for us.

But God shows his love for us in that while we were still sinners, Christ died for us. (Romans 5:8)

>> Who are five people you really love? If you had to sacrifice the life of one of them so the other four could live, who would you choose? Seems unbearable to even think about, doesn't it?

>> Who is one person you know that you can't stand to be around? If this person were dying and could live only by receiving a heart transplant from you, would you die to save his or her life?

You get the point: God's love is unconditional. He sacrificed His only Son on the cross for you. Jesus' love is amazing. He suffered and died on the cross so we could live.

In the space below, write a note to God or draw a picture that expresses how you feel about His love for you.

CHRIST'S CROSS . . .

Removes the penalty for our sins (sin is anything that pulls you away from God).

[13] You were dead because of your sins and because your sinful nature was not yet cut away. Then God made you alive with Christ, for he forgave all our sins. [14] He canceled the record of the charges against us and took it away by nailing it to the cross. (Colossians 2:13-14, NLT)

>> Write down a list of ten sins (the first ones that come to your mind) that you are or were struggling with.

....

....

....

....

....

....

....

....

....

....

Christ's death on the cross pays the penalty for our sins if we are willing to repent and receive His forgiveness.

Imagine this list being nailed to the cross the day Jesus died for you. Now take a big black marker and put a huge X over this list. Thank Jesus that He forgave *all* your sins!

CHRIST'S CROSS . . .

Offers God's gift of salvation to us through His grace.

> [8]*For by grace you have been saved through faith. And this is not your own doing; it is the gift of God,* [9]*not a result of works, so that no one may boast. (Ephesians 2:8-9)*

Grace is a word that the Bible uses to describe something amazing about God. Simply put, God's grace is expressed to us whenever He gives us something good that we don't deserve. This grace is a gift from God.

God's gift of salvation through Jesus lasts forever.

>> Finish this prayer for yourself: *Jesus, because I have received You as a gift into my life, I know*

....

....

CHRIST'S CROSS . . .

Secures eternal life for us now and in heaven.

> [11]*And this is the testimony, that God gave us eternal life, and this life is in his Son.* [12]*Whoever has the Son has life; whoever does not have the Son of God does not have life.* [13]*I write these things to you who believe in the name of the Son of God that you may know that you have eternal life. (1 John 5:11-13)*

>> Write a brief description of how, when, and where you said *yes* to Jesus or when you came to realize that you were trusting Christ (and Christ alone) to forgive you and take you to heaven.

....

....

....

CHRIST'S CROSS . . .

Starts a new identity for us in Christ.

Therefore, if anyone is in Christ, he is a new creation. The old has passed away; behold, the new has come. (2 Corinthians 5:17)

Talk about a complete makeover! When you received God's gift of salvation through Christ, you became a brand-new person! You are not the same anymore. Maybe you're not sure that you're seeing it yet, but God does.

With your new identity, remember that Jesus will help you live out the reality of being a new person. This means that as you grow in your relationship with Christ, you will experience God's power bringing about Christlike changes in your thoughts, attitudes, and actions.

>> Write down three changes you have already noticed since you became a brand-new person, "a new creation" in Christ:

BEFORE   **AFTER**

1. ....

2. ....

3. ....

Use words or a picture to illustrate the difference in your life since you started your relationship with Jesus Christ.

My Story

My name is Theresa. Recently I approached my friend Jenna to talk. Jenna is one of these people who seems to have it all together. Not in a snotty way, but more like safe and honest and real. You know what I mean? It wasn't safe to talk to my parents or teachers or even my youth pastor at church. They would be so disappointed in me.

So I told Jenna my story—the whole ugly deal. She was kind and a little shocked. Jenna didn't seem disappointed, and I knew she wouldn't tell anyone else.

My story is messy . . . before becoming a Christian I got pregnant and had a baby. God used that part of my story to bring me to the point of trusting Him for forgiveness and loving Him for giving me purpose and security. God helped me to see that He was worth trusting more than my boyfriends. But then a new guy came along and—well, I messed up badly this time!

Now Jenna knows. I'm pregnant again. Telling my mom is going to be so hard. But it seems even harder to trust that God can forgive me and love me *again*!

My story seemed so horrible, until Jenna reminded me about God's Story—*again*! God's Story contains the Good News (the gospel) that Jesus connects my life story to His story no matter what! It goes like this:

>> God loves me and created me for a good *relationship* with Him. No matter how badly I mess up, He wants my story with His story!

But God shows his love for us in that while we were still sinners, Christ died for us. (Romans 5:8)

[4]He chose us in him before the foundation of the world, that we should be holy and blameless before him. In love [5]he predestined us for adoption . . . through Jesus Christ, according to the purpose of his will. (Ephesians 1:4-5)

>> I often *resist* my relationship with God.

For all have sinned and fall short of the glory of God. (Romans 3:23)

>> Despite how I sometimes ignore God, Jesus lived, died, and rose from the dead to *restore* my relationship with God.

That's what Christ did definitively: suffered because of others' sins, the Righteous One for the unrighteous ones. He went through it all—was put to death and then made alive—to bring us to God. (1 Peter 3:18, The Message)

>> When I respond to the Lord Jesus Christ, my relationship with God grows.

But to all who did receive him, who believed in his name, he gave the right to become children of God. (John 1:12)

[6]Therefore, as you received Christ Jesus the Lord, so walk in him, [7]rooted and built up in him and established in the faith, just as you were taught, abounding in thanksgiving. (Colossians 2:6-7)

My story is messy, muddled, and sometimes in disarray. Thank God that He is ready to love me again and again and again. And thank God for Jenna too!

Our Story

God intended for His family to live and love in community. This is much more than attending a church service. It's about the Body of Christ working and serving together and caring for one another.

>> If you were involved in a church before you became a follower of Jesus, what was it like for you? Good? Bad? Describe your experience.

....

....

....

Take a look at an "our story" passage from the Bible. Read Colossians 3:10-17 one verse at a time, and answer the questions.

Put on the new self, which is being renewed in knowledge after the image of its creator. (Colossians 3:10)

>> This takes us back to becoming a brand-new person when we receive Christ as our Savior. Where does this new identity come from?

....

....

....

>> What would a church be like if everyone in it put on the new self every day?

....

....

....

Here there is not Greek and Jew, circumcised and uncircumcised, barbarian, Scythian, slave, free; but Christ is all, and in all. (Colossians 3:11)

>> In your new relationship with Jesus, what should your attitude be about the race, education, and social status of other people?

....

....

Put on then, as God's chosen ones, holy and beloved, compassionate hearts, kindness, humility, meekness, and patience. (Colossians 3:12)

>> How should followers of Jesus treat others?

....

....

Bearing with one another and, if one has a complaint against another, forgiving each other; as the Lord has forgiven you, so you also must forgive. (Colossians 3:13)

>> What should a Christ follower always be ready to do?

....

....

And above all these put on love, which binds everything together in perfect harmony. (Colossians 3:14)

>> How could "put[ting] on love" be done in some practical ways through a local church?

....

....

>> List three ways you could be an example of this love with other followers of Jesus.

....

....

....

And let the peace of Christ rule in your hearts, to which indeed you were called in one body. And be thankful. (Colossians 3:15)

>> What would you envision happening in a local church if people were to do this?

....

....

....

Let the word of Christ dwell in you richly, teaching and admonishing one another in all wisdom, singing psalms and

hymns and spiritual songs, with thankfulness in your hearts to God. (Colossians 3:16)

>> How do you express your thankfulness to God?

....

....

....

And whatever you do, in word or deed, do everything in the name of the Lord Jesus, giving thanks to God the Father through him. (Colossians 3:17)

>> This is about being a representative of Jesus. How would your daily life be different if you practiced this every day? How would it affect others around you?

....

....

....

The Story Continues

BECOME LIKE JESUS

God's Word makes it clear that the goal for every follower of Jesus is to become more Christlike. *The Living Bible* paraphrases Colossians 3:10 this way: *You are living a brand new kind of life that is continually learning more and more of what is right, and trying constantly to be more like Jesus Christ who created this new life within you.*

>> List five ways you want to be more like Jesus.

1. ....

2. ....

3. ....

4. ....

5. ....

RELY ON JESUS

Trust Christ to make changes happen in your life. In the same way that only Jesus can save you from your sins, only He can provide the power you need to become more like Him.

> *Being confident of this, that he who began a good work in you will carry it on to completion until the day of Christ Jesus. (Philippians 1:6, NIV)*

>> Write down three steps you would like to take every day to learn to rely on Jesus in order to become more like Him.

1. ....

2. ....

3. ....

CONFESS TO JESUS

You probably have already discovered that life didn't suddenly become perfect when you met Jesus. You still have problems at home and with your friends. Life is still complicated and messy. You will still struggle with sin every day. Some days you will do well at walking away from sin, and on other days you will leap right into it.

The difference is that Jesus is now in the middle of your complicated, messy life. He knows that you struggle with sin, and He knows that you will never be perfect or have a perfect life on earth. As a child in God's family, you will at times mess up and sin. But God's love for you is so great that He will forgive you! That's grace!

> *If we confess our sins, he is faithful and just to forgive us our sins and to cleanse us from all unrighteousness. (1 John 1:9)*

Remember that it's not helpful to make excuses for our sins because our loving heavenly Father already sees every move we make. Instead we should confess (which means to agree with God) our sins to God. He will forgive us completely because when Jesus died on the cross, He paid the penalty for every sin we will ever commit. What a great God of *grace*!

{ CHAPTER 2

How Do I Know God Loves Me?

EXPERIENCING GOD'S GREAT LOVE STORY

Life is loaded with images of love! By the time we reach high school we've encountered a flood of superficial love images, many of which work against our deep desire for authentic, unconditional love. Take a minute to think about who or what has shaped your definition of love. Add your specific ideas to this list:

Influences That Define Love

Parents	Television	Music
....	....	....
....	....	....

It is basic human nature to desire love, but not the romance novel love or the "I love pizza and football" love. Instead God created us to receive intimate, all-knowing, committed love. We start looking for it soon after we're born. In the early 1980s, sociologists studied babies in Russian orphanages. Hundreds of infants had been abandoned, and the orphanages were terribly understaffed—they couldn't hire enough people to hold and snuggle the children. Many babies were simply left lying in cribs, receiving nothing but bottles and diaper changes—limited human contact. Others were held when workers had free hands. After watching these babies develop over the years, researchers saw that the infants who had *not* been held, rocked, or sung to were the first to die. The cause? A lack of love.

As horrible as that sounds, it's believable, right? In

fact, right now you probably can think of people who are dying from lack of love. Some are trying desperately to find love, doing what they think is necessary to receive the love they desire.

Try this. Using words and sketches, write or draw items used to seek love by the figures below. Use talk bubbles or props to illustrate the actions you have seen as people search for love.

The Problem

The methods we use to attract love often have the opposite effect. We end up feeling disappointed, used, and perhaps less loved. We pour money into certain clothing styles thinking that a look will draw love our way. When that doesn't work, we feel let down and experience emptiness without love. We hang out with a social group thinking, *Here's where I'll find love.* But when that doesn't happen, we lose hope and self-esteem.

Have you ever tried looking at a spectacular view through a dirty windshield? You know the beauty of nature is out there, behind the dirt and bugs, but you have to search beyond the gunk to see mountains, wildflowers, or ocean. In the same way, God's love for us is intense and majestic, but often we can't see it because of the dirt. You need to look beyond, past, the dirt of life to see God's love clearly.

>> What life experiences have influenced your understanding of love?

....

....

....

>> Which of your ideas or beliefs about love may be incorrect and call for change? What "insect stains" may be blurring your view?

....

....

....

>> In what ways does God's love differ from the world's understanding of love?

....

....

....

The Bible is God's great love story, and it is your direct connection to a clear view of His love. From His creating Adam and Eve to creating you, from His salvation of the Israelites to His capturing of your heart, God's love is alive. It's active, and it's pursuing you.

How can you be sure?

Dive into the Bible. Connect with God's Story, and develop a new perspective of love with no distortions or blemishes. No windshield wipers necessary. God's love for you is magnified within the pages of His Word.

God's Story

As you read the following story, notice that . . .

>> When Jesus stopped to rest during a journey, He met a Samaritan woman in the midst of her daily chores.
>> This woman had a reputation for sleeping around and lacking morals. She was an outcast in her community because of her loose lifestyle.
>> Rather than condemning this woman, Jesus sat down at the well and started a conversation.

[5]So he came to a town of Samaria called Sychar, near the field that Jacob had given to his son Joseph. [6]Jacob's well was there; so Jesus, wearied as he was from his journey, was sitting beside the well. It was about the sixth hour. [7]There came a woman of Samaria to draw water. Jesus said to her, "Give me a drink." [8](For his disciples had gone into the city to buy food.) [9]The Samaritan woman said to

him, "How is it that you, a Jew, ask for a drink from me, a woman of Samaria?" (For Jews have no dealings with Samaritans.) [10]Jesus answered her, "If you knew the gift of God, and who it is that is saying to you, 'Give me a drink,' you would have asked him, and he would have given you living water." [11]The woman said to him, "Sir, you have nothing to draw water with, and the well is deep. Where do you get that living water? [12]Are you greater than our father Jacob? He gave us the well and drank from it himself, as did his sons and his livestock." [13]Jesus said to her, "Everyone who drinks of this water will be thirsty again, [14]but whoever drinks of the water that I will give him will never be thirsty again. The water that I will give him will become in him a spring of water welling up to eternal life." [15]The woman said to him, "Sir, give me this water, so that I will not be thirsty or have to come here to draw water."

[16]Jesus said to her, "Go, call your husband, and come here." [17]The woman answered him, "I have no husband." Jesus said to her, "You are right in saying, 'I have no husband'; [18]for you have had five husbands, and the one you now have is not your husband. What you have said is true."

[19]The woman said to him, "Sir, I perceive that you are a prophet. [20]Our fathers worshiped on this mountain, but you say that in Jerusalem is the place where people ought to worship." [21]Jesus said to her, "Woman, believe me, the hour is coming when neither on this mountain nor in Jerusalem will you worship the Father. [22]You worship what you do not know; we worship what we know, for salvation is from the Jews. [23]But the hour is coming, and is now here, when the true worshipers will worship the Father in spirit and truth, for the Father is seeking such people to worship him. [24]God is spirit, and those who worship him must worship in spirit and truth." [25]The woman said to him, "I know that Messiah is coming (he who is called Christ). When he comes, he will tell us all things." [26]Jesus said to her, "I who speak to you am he."

[27]Just then his disciples came back. They marveled that he was talking with a woman, but no one said, "What do you seek?" or, "Why are you talking with her?"

[28]So the woman left her water jar and went away into town and said to the people, [29] "Come, see a man who told me all that I ever did. Can this be the Christ?" [30]They went out of the town and were coming to him. . . .

[39]Many Samaritans from that town believed in him because of the woman's testimony, "He told me all that I ever did." [40]So when the Samaritans came to him, they asked him to stay with them, and he stayed there two days. [41]And many more believed because of his word. [42]They said to the woman, "It is no longer because of what you said that we believe, for we have heard for ourselves, and we know that this is indeed the Savior of the world." (John 4:5-30, 39-42)

Investigate the Story

The woman at the well had a reputation, a life gone wrong, and a past that made her an outcast. Not only were women considered lowly, but multiple marriages and divorces were unacceptable in her society. When Jesus stopped His journey and connected with this woman, He revealed the nature of God's love. It's a love that walks right into daily routines, blows away society's expectations, and embraces individual hearts. Jesus' love did not stop because this woman had a poor reputation. His love did not stop because of her culture. His love did not stop because she lived with a man who was not her husband. Nothing the woman had done or would do could stop the love Jesus had for her.

The same goes for you.

Mr. Mac has a student named Sid in his fourth period geometry class. Monday through Friday at 12:28 the bell rings for lunch. Everyone else is jammed up at the door, ready to spring toward food and soda machines. Not Sid. He doesn't even start packing his stuff until the room has emptied. By the time he gets to the lunchroom, so many people are standing in the food lines that he gives up. Head down, Sid circles the room a few times but looks at no one. Eventually he ends up in the doorway to his fifth period class, where he stands alone and eats a banana. It's like he wants to be alone.

Read the following questions, and record your responses in the space provided.

>> What does Sid have in common with the woman from Samaria?

....

....

....

>> When have you felt like an outcast or that no one cares about you?

....

....

....

>> How does Jesus feel about outcasts?

....

....

Perhaps you have days like Sid from Mr. Mac's class. You avoid people, protect your heart, keep to yourself, and expect to be alone. Maybe you are like the Samaritan. You don't feel worthy of love. No one has ever shown you real love, so you give up, go about your daily routine, and expect to be alone.

Stop your routine. Lift up your head. Pay attention. Jesus wants to love you.

God's love moves directly into daily life and embraces you right where you are. The woman at the well simply expects to complete her routine of tedious chores in isolation as usual. Instead she meets Jesus. Rather than pointing out her sin or making her feel judged, Jesus does as He always does—He approaches relationships with tenderness. While the woman thought she just needed water for daily chores and meals, Jesus knew that her needs went deeper.

Answer the following questions:

>> What did Jesus know that the woman at the well really needed?

....

....

....

>> What needs do you have that are not obvious to everyone?

....

....

....

Jesus connected with the woman by discovering her story. He knew her completely and yet wanted her to trust Him and tell the truth about her past. God's love sees deep into hearts and reveals truth. Because Jesus connected in a loving way, the woman at the well felt safe and was willing to expose her true need.

Discover More of the Story

¹⁴For this reason I bow my knees before the Father, ¹⁵from whom every family in heaven and on earth is named, ¹⁶that according to the riches of his glory he may grant you to be strengthened with power through his Spirit in your inner being, ¹⁷so that Christ may dwell in your hearts through faith—that you, being rooted and grounded in love, ¹⁸may have strength to comprehend with all the saints what is the breadth and length and height and depth, ¹⁹and to know the love of Christ that surpasses knowledge, that you may be filled with all the fullness of God. (Ephesians 3:14-19)

God's love is *adoptive* (verses 14-15).

Circle the word *family* in the above passage. When you respond to Jesus by recognizing that He is God, you become part of God's family. You are an adopted brother or sister of Jesus and a child of God.

>> God has adopted you. Describe what it means to you to be in His family.

....

....

God's love is *personal* (verses 16-18).

In the passage above, write your name over the word *you* each time it appears. When Jesus loved the woman at the well, it was one on one. God's love is focused on individuals. That includes you!

>> What do these verses say God wants to give you?

....

....

....

God's love is *immeasurable* (verse 19).

>> The deepest point in the ocean is the Marianas Trench. It's 10,923 meters deep (that's 35,838 feet—almost seven miles!). God's love runs deeper.

>> The highest mountain peak on earth is Mount Everest, which is 8,850 meters high—more than 29,000 feet. God's love stretches higher.

>> How far is the east from the west? They reach on forever and never meet. God's love reaches further.

>> Describe God's love for you.

....

....

....

Nothing—*nothing*—can separate you from the love of God. No sin you have committed and no attitude you can adopt will diminish the love that God has for you.

> [38]*For I am sure that neither death nor life, nor angels nor rulers, nor things present nor things to come, nor powers,* [39]*nor height nor depth, nor anything else in all creation, will be able to separate us from the love of God in Christ Jesus our Lord.* (Romans 8:38-39)

My Story

Alcohol became my friend when I was fourteen. It was casual at first, not like some kid on TV at a raging party. Drinking alone was my preference. By sixteen it was hard alcohol that kept me company. Skipping classes and staying numb was my way of life. There were girls, parties, and partners in addiction. I pursued the dark edges of witchcraft and lied to my family.

I remember the moment love stepped in. A guy at work, Darren, shared lunch breaks and watched football in the staff lounge with me. Darren was clean, but he never judged me.

One day Darren told me that he was worried about me. He thought I looked tired and sick. I told him it had been a late night. When he asked why, I told him straight out, "I drink a lot." He said he had friends in AA and asked if I wanted to try it. Obviously I didn't want to, but he was a good guy, so I humored him.

It was at my first Alcoholics Anonymous meeting that I heard about the love of God. A recovering addict stood up and talked about how the power of Jesus in his heart helped him walk away from the liquor aisle in the grocery store. He said, "I really wanted that drink. I was pacing the aisle, looking at all the bottles and remembering the tastes. But I could hear God's voice telling me that He loved me and that He had a better life for me, so I walked out of the store."

The speaker seemed sincere, but it's pretty hard to believe that Jesus would want anything to do with me. I mean, my life is dark, and I like it that way. This world is too filled with pain and suffering to believe God is involved. But man, when that guy talked about hearing the voice of Jesus, I got chills. I swear I heard something in my own ears; it creeped me out. It was weird, but I was intrigued, so I went back a week later.

There was a Bible-reading at the next meeting. I'd been drinking that day, so I sat in the back row. When the guy read the words, it was like he was talking to me. *. . . but God shows his love for us in that while we were still sinners, Christ died for us* (Romans 5:8).

I was a drunken guy at an AA meeting. And Jesus died for me even though I was a mess.

My name's Jay. I haven't had a drink since the night I realized Jesus died for me. Jesus loves me right where I am. I know it's true because only Jesus could take this nasty addiction and use it to draw me close to Him. I totally depend on Him for every moment of my life. He shows His love for me by turning my addiction into a connecting place between Him and me. I need Him. He knows it, and now so do I.

Our Story

Have you seen Russian stacking dolls? They're called *matryoshka* and are made from hollowed-out wood carved into a doll shape. Hold one in your hand and you feel it rattle, as though something is inside. On closer examination, you find that the doll opens up, and inside you find a smaller, similarly shaped doll. Shake this second doll and you become aware that there is more to it. You open it and find yet another, smaller carved figurine. Again you rattle the doll and are assured there is yet another level to this attraction. It keeps getting deeper. You're engaged in the fun now. Shake, open, discover; go again. Eventually the smallest figure is discovered in the center of the doll, but even then you wonder, could there be more?

With Jesus, there is always more.

Think back to His encounter with the Samaritan woman at the well.

>> She was captured by His approach, but there's more . . .
>> In the midst of conversation she found that Jesus knew her story, but there's even more . . .
>> Jesus did not condemn her, but He showed love by listening. Still more love—there is always more with Jesus.

The layers of God's love keep unfolding. And like Russian stacking dolls, we begin to anticipate more. What will come next in this great love story?

Once again, read the end of the story and answer the questions below.

28So the woman left her water jar and went away into town and said to the people, 29 "Come, see a man who told me all that I ever did. Can this be the Christ?" 30They went out of the town and were coming to him. . . .

39Many Samaritans from that town believed in him because of the woman's testimony, "He told me all that I ever did." 40So when the Samaritans came to him, they asked him to stay with them, and he stayed there two days. 41And

many more believed because of his word. 42They said to the woman, "It is no longer because of what you said that we believe, for we have heard for ourselves, and we know that this is indeed the Savior of the world." (John 4:28-42)

>> What was the woman's response when Jesus identified Himself?

....

....

>> How did her community react when she shared the news?

....

....

As Jesus met the woman's needs and filled her with living water, she became so full that love overflowed! Running back to town with the good news, everyone saw in her God's love—pouring into her, filling her up, and overflowing to others. When the woman's friends and neighbors encountered Jesus, we see yet another layer to God's far-reaching love!

We don't know what happened to the people in that village in the months following the woman's encounter with Jesus, but we have a hint of a new community beginning to develop. It's the kind of community God wants for all of His children. The Bible calls this fellowship, which is a union of people who are connected by their love for Jesus and their love for each other. People who lovingly help one another to . . .

>> . . . admit their sin and expect mercy.

>> . . . feel encouraged when suffering.

>> . . . develop spiritual gifts.

>> . . . grow in faith and learn together.

>> . . . experience an authentic loving family.

Living water flows from Jesus to us and from us to others. It's like those stacking dolls; another level of God's love is revealed each time we connect with other believers.

You don't go to a well just to look at the water. You reach in, soak it up, get all you need and more! That's the way of Jesus—overflowing, everlasting love.

List three Christians with whom you will connect this week for prayer, encouragement, and accountability. Be specific about where and when you will meet.

Who	Where and When
....	....
....	....
....	....

The Story Continues

Right now find a silent space to spend some time with Jesus. Some people find solitude in the mountains; some choose the ocean; some go to a nature preserve or park. Perhaps you have a space in your room where you can sit and focus without distraction. Picture yourself sitting or perhaps kneeling as you speak with God. Imagine Jesus standing beside you. As you pray, you sense His presence with you. As you turn to Him, see the scars on His wrists. It's hard to look at His face, but picture that you do, and as you make eye contact, you see the marks along His forehead where a crown of thorns dug into His skin. Those marks remind you of the pain that He went through because of His love for you.

Jesus says,

"I tell you the truth, whoever hears my word and believes him who sent me has eternal life and will not be condemned; he has crossed over from death to life." (John 5:24, NIV)

"Come to me, all of you who are weary and carry heavy burdens, and I will give you rest." (Matthew 11:28, NLT)

"God shows his love for us in that while we were still sinners, Christ died for us." (Romans 5:8)

Read the following passages, and pay attention to God-style love. Use a notebook to record a summary of what you read and how God shows love in different ways to different people.

>> Deuteronomy 7:7-9—
   Who does God love and how?

   ....

>> Joshua 1:5—
   Who does God love and how?

   ....

>> Nehemiah 1:1–6:16—
   Who does God love and how?

   ....

>> Matthew 19:13-15—
   Who does God love and how?

   ....

>> John 11—
   Who does God love and how?

   ....

>> Luke 23:39-43—
   Who does God love and how?

   ....

>> John 3:16—
   Who does God love and how?

   ....

>> Luke 19:1-10—
   Who does God love and how?

   ....

>> John 8:3-11—
   Who does God love and how?

   ....

{ **CHAPTER 3**

What Is God Like?

LEARNING THE TRUTH ABOUT THE TRINITY

Warm up your brain cells with the Sudoku puzzles in the next column. Complete the grid so that every row, column, and 3 x 3 box contains the numbers 1 through 9 (no repeats).

God's Story

Jesus not only showed His disciples that He was God in the flesh, but He also taught them about the other two persons who also are the one, true, living God—God the

Father and God the Holy Spirit. Christians call this three-in-one God the Trinity.

8		6			2
	4	5		1	
		7			3
	9		4		6
2					8
7		1		5	
3			9		
	1	8		9	
4		2			5

SUPER TOUGH

5					2
	8	6			
4			1	7	
3					5
	9		7	1	
2		8			6
	6	3			8
			9	2	
7					4

VERY TOUGH

Jesus spoke to His disciples about His connection to God the Father and God the Holy Spirit just before His arrest and crucifixion.

[8]Philip said to him, "Lord, show us the Father, and it is enough for us." [9]Jesus said to him, "Have I been with you so long, and you still do not know me, Philip? Whoever has seen me has seen the Father. How can you say, 'Show us the Father'? [10]Do you not believe that I am in the Father and the Father is in me? The words that I say to you I do not speak on my own authority, but the Father who dwells in

me does his works. ¹¹Believe me that I am in the Father and the Father is in me, or else believe on account of the works themselves. . . .

¹⁵"If you love me, you will keep my commandments. ¹⁶And I will ask the Father, and he will give you another Helper, to be with you forever, ¹⁷even the Spirit of truth, whom the world cannot receive, because it neither sees him nor knows him. You know him, for he dwells with you and will be in you.

¹⁸"I will not leave you as orphans; I will come to you. ¹⁹Yet a little while and the world will see me no more, but you will see me. Because I live, you also will live. ²⁰In that day you will know that I am in my Father, and you in me, and I in you. ²¹Whoever has my commandments and keeps them, he it is who loves me. And he who loves me will be loved by my Father, and I will love him and manifest myself to him." ²²Judas (not Iscariot) said to him, "Lord, how is it that you will manifest yourself to us, and not to the world?" ²³Jesus answered him, "If anyone loves me, he will keep my word, and my Father will love him, and we will come to him and make our home with him. ²⁴Whoever does not love me does not keep my words. And the word that you hear is not mine but the Father's who sent me.

²⁵"These things I have spoken to you while I am still with you. ²⁶But the Helper, the Holy Spirit, whom the Father will send in my name, he will teach you all things and bring to your remembrance all that I have said to you. ²⁷Peace I leave with you; my peace I give to you. Not as the world gives do I give to you. Let not your hearts be troubled, neither let them be afraid." (John 14:8-27)

Investigate the Story

>> Jesus' disciples expected Him to use His power and popularity to lead a political revolt.

>> Jesus spoke with authority and wisdom like God. He also healed sick people, controlled nature, and even raised people from the dead. Only God can do that, right?

>> Jesus' disciples had lots of questions:

Was He really God, the Messiah who would establish God's Kingdom on earth?

How soon would all this happen?

>> What have you learned about Jesus during the last year? Who do you think He is?

....

....

....

Just before being arrested and crucified, Jesus explained

to His disciples that He and God the Father are equally the one, true, living God who exists in three distinct forms.

God the Father in heaven and Jesus the Son on earth are one and the same. When you see and hear Jesus, you are seeing and hearing God.

Just like the disciples, we were created by God, made in His image, and made to live forever. Our bodies will die, but our spirits will live on. Jesus is the God-man. He lived here on earth in a human body for thirty-three years to tell us about God and His love for us and to die on the cross to pay for the sins of those who would believe in Him. This act of love makes it possible for everyone who believes in Him and follows Him to be forgiven and live with God forever. This is God's great plan of redemption.

In this passage we see Philip, the disciple of Jesus, looking for assurance. He wanted to believe this was true. He believed in God, and he asked Jesus to show them the Father so he could believe that Jesus truly was God's Son. Jesus told him, "If you have seen me, then you have seen the Father." Philip and the disciples were looking at and talking to God living on earth.

>> What important questions about God and His plan for the world and His plan for you would you like to ask Jesus?

....

....

....

....

Like most people, Philip and the other disciples wanted to know where they had come from and where they would be going. Jesus answered their question. He was the link to their origins and to their future.

Jesus spoke about His death to the disciples. That kind of talk frightened them. They wondered what they would do if He were dead and gone. How would they know where to go, and who would help them?

Jesus promised that after His return to heaven, He would send God the Holy Spirit (the third person of the

Trinity) into the world. The Holy Spirit, the Comforter, would be with them and in them.

God the Spirit is everywhere, all over the earth at the same time. The disciples and in fact all persons who follow Jesus will never be alone because the Holy Spirit lives within them. The Holy Spirit comforts us, encourages us, and teaches us how to worship God and serve Him.

The disciples were scared, just like you and I would be. But their future and ours are secure because the Holy Spirit is here to help us. God is with us every minute of our lives.

Spell this out in capital letters: THE HOLY SPIRIT IS A PERSON. He is not enthusiasm. He is not courage. He is not energy. He is not the personification of all good qualities, like Jack Frost is the personification of cold weather. Actually the Holy Spirit is not the personification of anything. He is a Person. He has will and intelligence. He has hearing. He has knowledge and sympathy and ability to love and see and think. He can hear, speak, desire, grieve and rejoice. He is a Person. (A. W. Tozer, *The Counselor*)

>> What have you learned about the Holy Spirit since you gave your life to Jesus?

....

....

....

....

>> In what ways has the Holy Spirit been guiding you and helping you since you became a follower of Jesus?

....

....

....

....

....

Discover More of the Story

The Bible describes the one true God acting in three distinct persons.

> ²⁶*Then God said, "Let us make man in our image, after our likeness. . . ." ²⁷So God created man in his own image, in the image of God he created him; male and female he created them. (Genesis 1:26-27)*

>> In this passage God is described by the words "us" and "our" to show the three persons of the Trinity at the moment of creation bringing the earth and all living things into being.

>> God is one God who lives and acts in three distinct persons: God the Father, God the Son, and God the Holy Spirit.

>> This three-in-one God created the earth and everything in it, including men and women.

Read Genesis 1:26-27 again, and circle the words "us" and "our."

> *For you formed my inward parts;*
> *you knitted me together in my mother's womb.*
> *I praise you, for I am fearfully and wonderfully made.*
> *Wonderful are your works;*
> *my soul knows it very well.*
> *My frame was not hidden from you,*
> *when I was being made in secret,*
> *intricately woven in the depths of the earth.*
> *Your eyes saw my unformed substance;*
> *in your book were written, every one of them,*
> *the days that were formed for me,*
> *when as yet there were none of them.*
> *How precious to me are your thoughts, O God!*
> *How vast is the sum of them! (Psalm 139:13-17)*

>> Your life is part of God's great plan. Through the actions of your parents, He created you! You can give thanks and praise to God every day for giving you life.

>> God made you to be in step with Him every moment of your life.

>> How does it make you feel to know that you have a big part in God's plans?

....

....

....

....

19On the evening of that day, the first day of the week, the doors being locked where the disciples were for fear of the Jews, Jesus came and stood among them and said to them, "Peace be with you." 20When he had said this, he showed them his hands and his side. Then the disciples were glad when they saw the Lord. 21Jesus said to them again, "Peace be with you. As the Father has sent me, even so I am sending you." 22And when he had said this, he breathed on them and said to them, "Receive the Holy Spirit." (John 20:19-22)

>> Before Jesus left this earth after His death on the cross and His resurrection from the dead, He promised His followers they would not be alone.

>> Physically Jesus was leaving Planet Earth, but the third person of the Trinity—the Holy Spirit—would come to be with them.

>> If you were a disciple of Jesus, how might you react to what He told you about the Holy Spirit's coming?

....

....

....

....

By this we know that we abide in him and he in us, because he has given us of his Spirit. (1 John 4:13)

Do you not know that you are God's temple and that God's Spirit dwells in you? (1 Corinthians 3:16)

>> Every person who believes and follows Jesus has the Holy Spirit living in him or her.

>> You are never alone. God is always with you.

>> How does it make you feel that you will never be alone?

....

....

....

....

My Story

Hi, I'm Jarred.

I became a Christian six months ago.

At summer camp.

It's been hard.

First three months were good.
Like riding a big wave of God.
Last three months a different story.
Fighting lots of temptation.
Giving in.
Feeling like a failure.
Feeling empty and disappointed with myself.
Hard to talk about it with others.
If it's my job to make myself a better person
I'm failing badly.
When I left summer camp
My focus was on Jesus.
Cool guy.
Guts and powerful love.
His death and resurrection.
How He treated His disciples.
I wanted to be part of all that.
Now I feel I am letting Him down.
Don't want to look Him in the face.
I was ready to bail.
Went to church over Christmas.
Saw something different.

I had been ignoring a lot of the Bible.
Whenever I thought about God
He seemed like the old guy in heaven.
Like the principal of the school.
A stern guy who is focused on the rules.
The Christmas story showed me
Jesus coming to earth was God's plan
To find and rescue guys like me.
The whole Bible is filled with
God working out His plan.
Never giving up on us.
I never thanked Him for it
Until that night.
The Holy Spirit scared me.
Was he a ghost or what?
I didn't understand.
Hard to relate to someone without a face.
Another Christmas surprise.
Those mysterious moments we sing about
Holding candles in church.
The Holy Spirit was all over that.
Making a miracle baby 2,000 years ago.

Giving courage to teenage parents.
None of it happens without God.
Same Holy Spirit oozed out of Jesus.
Helped Him resist temptation.
Gave courage when facing death.
Raised Him from the dead.
Transformed disciples.
Launched the church.
Turned the world upside down.
Same Holy Spirit came to me
When I prayed to Jesus.
Waited patiently for me to wake up,
Ready to fill me with hope and power.
Endless supply of God available
For a lifelong journey.
Yielding to become like Jesus.
Praising God forever.

Our Story

God wants us to get together with other believers—to learn to praise and worship Him with others.

In God's master plan Jesus used His ministry time on earth to start His Church, where people from all backgrounds and experiences would gather together to worship God the Father in spirit and truth. This new Church exploded in rapid growth in Jerusalem when God the Holy Spirit came into the world after Jesus returned to heaven.

The global Church is called the Body of Christ. Each believer and follower of Jesus is given spiritual gifts (abilities) by God the Holy Spirit to be used to build up others and the Church. We learn how to better hear and respond to the Holy Spirit when we gather with other Christians.

Ordinary people with little education and training became dynamic leaders empowered by God the Holy Spirit as they met together to worship God.

And whatever you do, in word or deed, do everything in the name of the Lord Jesus, giving thanks to God the Father through him. (Colossians 3:17)

>> It is good for followers of Jesus to get together regularly to worship God. Why is this better than only doing it individually and privately?

....

....

....

....

5For those who live according to the flesh set their minds on the things of the flesh, but those who live according to the Spirit set their minds on the things of the Spirit. 6To set the mind on the flesh is death, but to set the mind on the Spirit is life and peace. (Romans 8:5-6)

>> List some choices that lead to death.

....

....

....

>> Now list some choices that lead to life and peace.

....

....

....

....

Followers of Jesus in the early church encouraged and strengthened each other to make choices that led to life and peace, not death.

If we live by the Spirit, let us also walk by the Spirit. (Galatians 5:25)

The Story Continues

Learn more about God the Father and how to focus your worship on Him.

Express your praise and thanks to God, naming and recounting how you have experienced these character traits of God in your life.

God the Father is:

>> eternal—without beginning or end
>> always truthful
>> fair and just
>> wise

>> full of mercy and love

>> faithful

>> unchanging

>> all-knowing and all-seeing

>> present everywhere

>> all-powerful

>> patient

>> holy

>> Creator and Redeemer—He made us and sent His Son to die for our sins.

>> Express your thoughts here as you spend time in worship.

....

....

....

>> Practice praying to God the Father like Jesus did, using these phrases from John 17 (and other Bible passages).

    praying for others and their needs

    praying for unity with other believers

    praying for God to be glorified

    praying for other believers to remain strong and committed to God

    praying for others to come to know and believe in God and His Son

>> Listen to your prayers. What do you need to say more often in your prayers?

....

....

....

>> Discover more about God the Holy Spirit. Open your life to let the Holy Spirit be more involved. In what parts of your life do you need the Holy Spirit to be more active and alive?

....

....

....

{ CHAPTER 4

What Does It Mean That the Bible Is True?

TRUSTING THE STORY, AS TOLD BY GOD

Some sports fans read *Sports Illustrated* every week and can tell you stories about star athletes, complete with statistics. Other individuals read *People Magazine* to get the scoop on the latest Hollywood romances and breakups. So where do we go to get an inside look at God and His actions and activities? The Bible. This amazing book is all about God's Story. As we read and understand the Bible, we will begin to personally connect to God and to learn how a relationship with Him can change our lives.

Here's a key Bible verse: *Do your best to present yourself to God as one approved, a worker who has no need to be ashamed, rightly handling the word of truth* (2 Timothy 2:15). "The word of truth" is the Bible, God's Word. "Rightly handling" this book may seem like a big challenge. It is, but it's important—and you can do it.

Here are some easy steps to help you begin:

>> Find a Bible, and locate the Table of Contents in the front.
>> Look up the verses below to discover some of the Bible's famous characters and hot topics.
>> Fill in the crossword puzzle.

Crossword Clues

Look up the Bible passages to determine the clues. Then enter the correct word in the right spot in the puzzle.

Famous Bible Characters and Hot Topics Crossword Puzzle

Across: Bible Characters

CLUE

1 450 to 1 odds (1 Kings 18:22)

6 Suffered in silence (Job 2:11-13)

7 A singing cellmate (Acts 16:25)

8 Walked on water with Jesus (Matthew 14:29-30)

9 Brought the house down (Judges 16:28-30)

11 Thirsty divorcée (John 4:7, 13-18)

14 Paul's spiritual son (1 Timothy 1:18)

17 Got stoned (Acts 7:59-60)

19 His son was a spared sacrifice (Genesis 22:9-13)

21 Lions left him untouched (Daniel 6:19-23)

22 Operated a floating zoo (Genesis 7:1-5)

24 Made a fashion statement (Genesis 37:2-4)

27 A voice in the desert (John 1:19-27)

29 From shepherd to king (2 Samuel 7:8-9)

31 A reputation worth imitating (3 John 11-12)

32 The original first lady (Genesis 3:20)

33 The Savior (Matthew 1:21)

36 Performed a perfume pedicure (John 12:1-3)

37 Revelation revealed (Revelation 1:1-3)

38 Carried the stone tablets containing the Ten Commandments (Exodus 34:4)

Down: Bible Topics

CLUE

2 Proverbs 27:4

3 Isaiah 47:13-15

4 Matthew 26:38

5 Romans 6:3-4

7 Matthew 6:5-15

10 Ecclesiastes 5:10

12 Philippians 4:6-7

13 John 16:13

15 Came to warn Lot about God destroying Sodom and Gomorrah (Genesis 19:1-13)

16 Genesis 1:27

18 Philippians 3:20

20 Romans 6:23

23 1 John 1:9

25 1 Thessalonians 4:3-5

26 Proverbs 20:19

27 Matthew 7:1-2

28 Ephesians 5:18

30 1 Corinthians 7:12

34 Romans 3:23

35 1 Corinthians 13

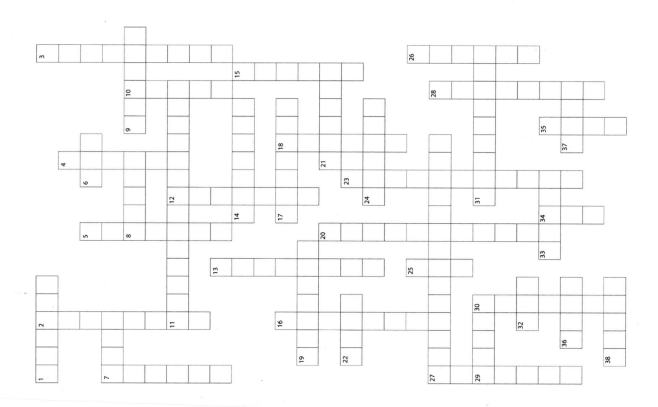

Congratulations. Whether you finish this now or later, you've discovered that you can find a verse in the Bible, read it, and live to tell about it. Maybe this book isn't so puzzling after all! (Check your answers at the end of this chapter.)

God's Story

Take a look at how Jesus put His knowledge of the Bible (often called Scripture) to work. In this story . . .

>> Jesus spent over a month in the desert.

>> Satan came along to tempt Jesus.

>> Jesus knew the temptations were wrong not only because He is God but because He knew the truth in Scripture.

¹Then Jesus was led up by the Spirit into the wilderness to be tempted by the devil. ²And after fasting forty days and forty nights, he was hungry. ³And the tempter came and said to him, "If you are the Son of God, command these stones to become loaves of bread." ⁴But he answered, "It is written, 'Man shall not live by bread alone, but by every word that comes from the mouth of God.'" ⁵Then the devil took him to the holy city and set him on the pinnacle of the temple ⁶and said to him, "If you are the Son of God,

throw yourself down, for it is written, 'He will command his angels concerning you,' and 'On their hands they will bear you up, lest you strike your foot against a stone.'" ⁷Jesus said to him, "Again it is written, 'You shall not put the Lord your God to the test.'" ⁸Again, the devil took him to a very high mountain and showed him all the kingdoms of the world and their glory. ⁹And he said to him, "All these I will give you, if you will fall down and worship me." ¹⁰Then Jesus said to him, "Be gone, Satan! For it is written, 'You shall worship the Lord your God and him only shall you serve.'" ¹¹Then the devil left him, and behold, angels came and were ministering to him. (Matthew 4:1-11)

Investigate the Story

Consider how Satan tempted Jesus to meet natural desires in the wrong way:

>> *"Command these stones to become loaves of bread."* What could be wrong with eating some bread? Jesus knew He was going without bread (He was fasting) to focus on God the Father. He could have made the bread, but it was not the right time for a miracle just to meet His physical desires.

>> *"Throw yourself down."* Satan next tempted Jesus to jump off a building just to prove that God would protect Him. Jesus

responded by saying that truly trusting in God means not putting Him through silly tests.

>> *"All these I will give you."* Just as he tempted Jesus, Satan tempts us to think that power, popularity, and possessions will make us more important. Jesus pointed out that "stuff" can get in the way of really worshiping God (acknowledging Him as God) and serving Him (making His priorities our priorities.)

Our world is very good at making us think that we need to:

>> look a certain way
>> do the right activities
>> have the right possessions
>> What examples can you think of when advertising pressures us to look, do, and have?

....

....

....

....

>> When do you see the pressure to look, do, and have show up in your friends?

....

....

....

....

>> When do you feel pressured to look, do, or have?

....

....

....

....

It is interesting that whether Satan was tempting Jesus to fulfill natural desires in a wrong way, to doubt His faith in God, or to seek worldly fame and fortune, Jesus' first line of defense was Scripture every time! As we read Scripture on a regular basis, we learn more and more truth, which will help us identify temptation as Satan's lies.

You may be asking, "But why the Bible? How do we know that the Bible is God's Word and is reliable truth?" Many resources address this question. Some are listed at the end of the chapter. If you check them out you discover that:

>> The writers of Scripture were leaders who were directed by God as they wrote.

>> These leaders were recognized by their peers as spokespersons for God.

>> Most of the New Testament writers were eyewitnesses of what they wrote.

>> The Scriptures were copied letter by letter with extreme care and accuracy.

>> Other historical documents support many of the stories in the Bible.

>> Archaeology continually digs up evidence to prove that stories in the Bible are true.

One significant fact is that the Bible *claims* to be God's Word. Jesus quoted a verse from the Old Testament when He said, *Man shall not live by bread alone, but by every word that comes from the mouth of God* (Matthew 4:4). He was clearly saying that the Old Testament, a large part of the Bible, had been spoken by God. Other Bible passages agree. One of them says, *For no prophecy was ever produced by the will of man, but men spoke from God as they were carried along by the Holy Spirit* (2 Peter 1:21).

We have an awesome opportunity to learn more about God, what He is like, and how He wants to interact with us.

Discover More of the Story

After buying a new car, the new owner reads the owner's manual to learn how to enjoy all the features of the car and how to keep it running well. Reading the Bible regularly is like that because it's an "owner's manual" for life. The Bible helps us learn more and more about the great features of our relationship with Jesus. Here's how the Bible can help us live.

16All Scripture is breathed out by God and profitable for **teaching**, *for* **reproof**, *for* **correction**, *and for* **training** *in righteousness, 17that the man of God may be competent,* **equipped** *for every good work. (2 Timothy 3:16-17)*

>> Look at the Bible passage above, and write down the five ways Scripture helps us, matching it to the paraphrases listed below.

.... *teaching us what is true*

.... *helping us realize what is wrong in our lives*

.... *straightening us out*

.... *helping us do what is right*

.... *equipping us fully to do good*

Let's spend a little time thinking about these five words:

TEACHING (TEACHING US WHAT IS TRUE)

I am but a pilgrim here on earth: how I need a map—and your commands are my chart and guide. (Psalm 119:19, TLB)

Just as a map helps us plan a trip, the Bible contains truth to guide decisions in life. The more we learn what Scripture teaches, the more the Bible becomes our personal map or GPS experience. It won't be as simple as entering your desired destination in life, then getting a printout of your future in detail:

>> You will go to Michigan State University.
>> You will major in electrical engineering.
>> You will marry your lab partner.
>> You will live in Charlotte, North Carolina.
>> You will have three children
     (two boys and a girl).
>> You will have a Labrador retriever named Spot.
>> You will enjoy walks on the beach.

Even though we don't get such a detailed map, the Bible addresses nearly every issue we face in life. We also discover God's love for us as we see how Jesus interacted with people. The more we love God and follow Jesus, the easier it will be to make good choices.

>> Write down those topics you would be interested in looking up in a study Bible.

....

....

....

....

....

REPROOF (HELPING US REALIZE WHAT IS WRONG IN OUR LIVES)

Many people think that following the directions in the Bible will somehow limit their freedom. The Bible only limits you to keep you from harm, both now and in the future.

Picture the boundaries set in Scripture as an underground pet fence. You don't install an electric pet fence to limit your dog's freedom. Your purpose is to free your dog from its ten-foot chain and set it free to explore the entire yard. God's "fences" help us experience the best life possible by keeping us from playing in traffic and getting run down by a medium-sized truck!

God is not like a police officer with a radar gun measuring how much fun you're having, just waiting to pull you over and make your life miserable. Rather, He is like a trusted counselor protecting you from harmful temptation. The Bible says, *No temptation has overtaken you that is not common to man. God is faithful, and he will not let you be tempted beyond your ability, but with the temptation he will also provide the way of escape, that you may be able to endure it* (1 Corinthians 10:13).

This one verse has many promises:

>> We are not alone in facing a particular temptation.
>> God protects us from temptation we can't handle.
>> Every temptation has a way out.

The Bible can help us realize when we do wrong, but God wants us to recognize temptation and take His way out!

>> What recent temptation did you face, recognize, and take the way of escape from? Describe the experience.

....

....

....

....

CORRECTION (STRAIGHTENING US OUT)

No one is perfect. The Bible says that everyone has sinned (Romans 3:23). Sin is our attitude of ignoring or resisting God. It leads us to miss the mark of how God wants us to live.

We may sin unintentionally, like when we go along with the crowd. We may sin intentionally, even rebelliously, by doing what we know is wrong. Either way we need to get straightened out and back on track. The Bible says that, once again, God is waiting to help: *If we confess our sins, he is faithful and just to forgive us our sins and to cleanse us from all unrighteousness* (1 John 1:9).

>> Why do you think we tend to walk around feeling guilty, instead of going to God and asking for forgiveness?

....

....

....

....

....

TRAINING IN RIGHTEOUSNESS (HELPING US DO WHAT IS RIGHT)

Your word is a lamp to my feet and a light to my path. (Psalm 119:105)

The more we stay connected to God and experience life with Him in control, the more we want to build a stronger relationship with Him. We can use the "light" of Scripture to illuminate our feet (who we are) and our "path" (where we are going).

>> Write down a few of your sports or hobbies that seemed really difficult for you at first, but as you trained and practiced them, they became one of your favorite things to do.

....

....

....

....

EQUIPPED FOR EVERY GOOD WORK (EQUIPPING US FULLY TO DO GOOD)

When God has changed us so much that we begin to treat others differently, life really gets interesting and fun! See Chapter 6 for some life-changing tips on how to love other people.

My Story

I'm Marie, and I'm now a high school senior. I received my first Bible for Christmas from my grandparents twelve years ago, when I was six years old. My Sunday school classes always studied something in the Bible, and the sermon was always explaining a passage of Scripture. In high school I was on the Bible quiz team. We would study together once a week and have a quiz meet every month. I would memorize an entire chapter of the Bible just to be ready to answer the maximum allowed five questions. I read the Bible cover to cover the first time while still in high school because my church challenged everyone to do it.

But then one day instead of just reading the Bible, I began to understand how much sense it made. I started believing the Bible. Then, as if believing wasn't enough, I started living it, and that has made all the difference. I've learned that:

>> God really does love me (John 3:16).

>> A soft answer really does stop an argument (Proverbs 15:1).

>> Prayer really does relieve stress and bring a sense of peace (Philippians 4:6-7).

>> I really do communicate better when I listen first and speak second (James 1:19).

>> And so much more.

At times you will read the Bible and think that a certain passage was written personally to you. Because it is God's word to us, it is more than just historical truth. It is truth meant to be personal. And sometimes it's just the point you are looking for! *For the word of God is living and active, sharper than any two-edged sword, piercing to the division of soul and of spirit, of joints and of marrow, and discerning the thoughts and intentions of the heart* (Hebrews 4:12).

At other times what you read in God's Word might seem arachaic or too difficult to understand. Please do not give up. Don't close the Bible and throw it across the room. Pray. Ask for help from God. Ask a trusted Christian friend to hear your questions and help you. Don't let yourself become overly fearful or angry with your struggles. God wants to help us understand and love His Word.

Our Story

The Bible is a big book written over a span of several thousand years. It takes a while to feel like it is making sense. We need to read it regularly ourselves, but it also helps to read it with others who might be able to help us understand and apply its truth. The Bible says: *[6]And now, just as you accepted Christ Jesus as your Lord, you must continue to follow him. [7]Let your roots grow down into him and draw up nourishment from him, so you will grow in faith, strong and vigorous in the truth you were taught* (Colossians 2:6-7, NLT).

Get involved in a church where . . .

>> Jesus is taught as the only way to have a relationship with God.
>> Sermons are based on God's truth found in the Bible.
>> The focus is helping you apply biblical truth to your daily life.

During the services, sit near the front and take notes on the teaching from God's Word. Use the bulletin or a notebook you bring for your notes. Highlight or underline key verses in your own Bible.

In addition to attending church, look for one smaller setting to study the Bible a little less formally. It may be a Sunday school class, a youth group, or a small group. In these smaller settings you will learn and interact with others who are on the same journey.

The Story Continues

John was one of the disciples who recorded the life of Jesus, which he witnessed firsthand. He explains why he selected the stories he included in his Gospel: *30Now Jesus did many other signs in the presence of the disciples, which are not written in this book; 31but these are written so that you may believe that Jesus is the Christ, the Son of God, and that by believing you may have life in his name* (John 20:30-31).

Learning the Bible is learning God's Story. Are you ready to get started? If so . . .

>> Ask a Christian friend to recommend a Bible geared toward your age.
>> Set a goal to read the Bible a few minutes every day.
>> Highlight or underline key verses.
>> Write down questions you have.
>> Start a journal, and answer these questions about the passage, story, or chapter you are reading.
   Is there a *truth* to obey? (If so, what is it?)
   Is there an *example* to follow? (If so, what is it?)
   Is there a *story* to remember? (If so, what is it?)

If you are reading the Bible for the first time, read these books first:

>> Mark—a short account of the life of Jesus
>> James—putting your faith into practice
>> Philippians—living a life of joy
>> John—great stories of Jesus' connecting to people
>> Proverbs—wise thoughts to live by

As you increase in biblical knowledge, you will gain confidence in your faith. You will find yourself being more comfortable talking about your relationship with God with your friends. You don't need to have all the answers. Just share with them what you are learning—maybe they will want to join in the fun!

Other resources to learn more about the Bible being trustworthy include:

>> *The Case for Faith* by Lee Strobel
>> *Evidence That Demands a Verdict* by Josh McDowell
>> *How to Read the Bible for All Its Worth* by Gordon Fee and Douglas Stuart

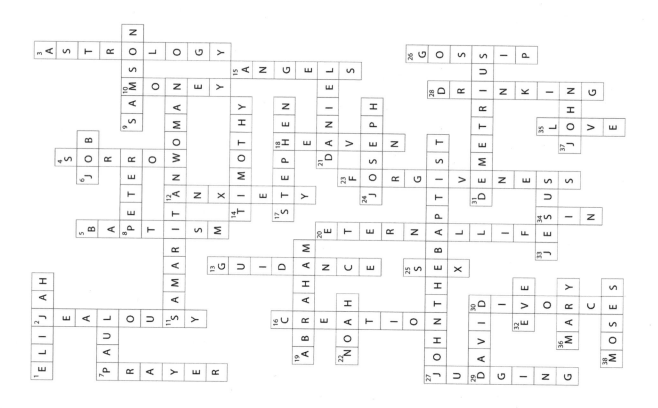

{ **CHAPTER 5**

How Can I Learn to Love God?
RESPONDING TO GOD'S LOVE FOR ME

Zits? A beautiful smile? Ears or a nose you wish you could change? Braces? Glasses?

Someone once said, "If God had a refrigerator, your picture would be on it." Imagine that! God, the Creator of the universe, loves you so much that you are front and center in His thoughts.

Hey, grab a picture of yourself. Any recent picture will do. Grab some tape or glue, and stick the picture right on the refrigerator drawn in the next column.

Now study that person. What do you see? Great hair?

>> Write down what you see as you look at that picture of yourself.

....

....

....

In the Old Testament of the Bible, God told His followers He would always remember them and that His love for them would never end.

15I will not forget you. 16Behold, I have engraved you on the palms of my hands. (Isaiah 49:15-16)

Just as He promised His people many years ago, God knows your name—you can be sure of that—and His love for you is unending. When you look at your picture, you probably see things you don't like. When God looks at you, He sees someone He deeply loves. Cool thought, huh? Your name known and remembered forever by the Creator of the universe!

We learn to love God when we realize how much He really loves us. So God's love for you is where your love for Him starts. When we think about how to love God, we have to start at the source.

The person in your picture has a story. Your story is made up of all the experiences you have had in life—your great memories, hard lessons, successes, failures, friendships, family, joys, and losses. All of this comprises who you are and who you are becoming. God started creating your story before you were born, and He will continue to write it for the rest of your life.

God's love for you is what connects His story to your story. Your love for God is what connects your story to His story.

Look at the picture of yourself one more time. God loves you so much that He has your picture on His "refrigerator." Do you ever wonder if there is anything you could ever do to make God change His mind about you?

God's Story

>> Peter was one of three disciples who had an especially tight relationship with Jesus. And yet Jesus explained that Peter would deny knowing Him: Will you lay down your life for me? Truly,

truly, I say to you, the rooster will not crow till you have denied me three times (John 13:38).

>> Although Peter didn't believe Jesus at the time, eventually he did actually deny knowing Christ, and not just once but three times.

The servant girl at the door said to Peter, "You also are not one of this man's disciples, are you?" He said, "I am not." (John 18:17)

Now Simon Peter was standing and warming himself. So they said to him, "You also are not one of his disciples, are you?" He denied it and said, "I am not." (John 18:25)

26One of the servants of the high priest, a relative of the man whose ear Peter had cut off, asked, "Did I not see you in the garden with him?" 27Peter again denied it, and at once a rooster crowed. (John 18:26-27)

>> As you read this next passage of Scripture, pay close attention to Jesus' response to Peter despite Peter's letting him down.

4Just as day was breaking, Jesus stood on the shore; yet the disciples did not know that it was Jesus. 5Jesus said to them, "Children, do you have any fish?" They answered him, "No." 6He said to them, "Cast the net on the right side of the boat, and you will find some." So they cast it, and now they were not able to haul it in, because of the quantity of fish.

7That disciple whom Jesus loved therefore said to Peter, "It is the Lord!" When Simon Peter heard that it was the Lord, he put on his outer garment, for he was stripped for work, and threw himself into the sea. 8The other disciples came in the boat, dragging the net full of fish, for they were not far from the land, but about a hundred yards off.

9When they got out on land, they saw a charcoal fire in place, with fish laid out on it, and bread. 10Jesus said to them, "Bring some of the fish that you have just caught." 11So Simon Peter went aboard and hauled the net ashore, full of large fish, 153 of them. And although there were so many, the net was not torn. 12Jesus said to them, "Come and have breakfast." Now none of the disciples dared ask him, "Who are you?" They knew it was the Lord. 13Jesus came and took the bread and gave it to them, and so with the fish. 14This was now the third time that Jesus was revealed to the disciples after he was raised from the dead.

15When they had finished breakfast, Jesus said to Simon Peter, "Simon, son of John, do you love me more than these?" He said to him, "Yes, Lord; you know that I love you." He said to him, "Feed my lambs." 16He said to him a second time, "Simon, son of John, do you love me?" He said to him, "Yes, Lord; you know that I love you." He said to him, "Tend my sheep." 17He said to him the third time, "Simon, son of John, do you love me?" Peter was grieved because he said to him the third time, "Do you love me?" and he said to him, "Lord, you know everything; you know that I love you." Jesus said to him, "Feed my sheep. 18Truly, truly, I say to you, when you were young, you used to dress yourself and walk wherever you wanted, but when you are old, you will stretch out your hands, and another will dress you and carry you where you do not want to go." [19](This he said to show by what kind of death he was to glorify God.) And after saying this he said to him, "Follow me." (John 21:4-19)

Investigate the Story

Put yourself in Peter's shoes. He had denied knowing his best friend. Now the friend was back. When Peter saw Jesus from the boat, Peter wasted no time getting to Him. As he swam and waded to shore, I wonder if Peter was trying to think of the best apology ever. How could he explain to Jesus his temporary gutless moments?

Surprisingly, Jesus didn't make Peter feel guilty, and He expressed no anger. Instead Jesus told Peter to join Him for breakfast. As they sat together, Jesus began to question Peter. "Do you love Me?" was his first question. Peter answered, "Yes, I love You."

If you were Jesus, you probably would have responded to Peter more like this: "Oh yeah? Then why did you deny knowing Me? Why are you such a coward? Some friend you are!"

But Jesus didn't say any of that. Instead He told Peter, "Feed My lambs." Three times Jesus asked Peter, "Do you love Me?"—once for each time that Peter had denied knowing Him.

Jesus was not trying to make Peter feel guilty. But He knew that a repentant Peter desperately needed forgiveness and renewed friendship. Jesus knew that Peter loved Him, but He wanted to give Peter the chance to publicly express that love.

Jesus loved Peter, and by calling him to feed His sheep and follow Him, he was expressing that love to Peter. When Jesus told Peter to "feed My sheep," he was saying in effect, "I still believe in you. You messed up, but you aren't hopeless. I still love you and still want to use you in people's lives."

In saying, "Follow Me," Jesus was reminding Peter of the time when He had first invited Peter to be His disciple, His follower. Jesus was telling Peter how to show love for God—by following Him and feeding His sheep. Instead of getting fired, Peter got a fresh start.

Peter was forgiven. Jesus still loved him. The depths of Peter's love at that moment must have been deeper than he could have ever imagined. The Son of God loved him, and because of that Peter couldn't help but love Him in return. The forgiveness and love that Peter experienced connected his story even more to God's Story. This encounter with Jesus caused Peter to love God more. In other words, Peter messed up, but his picture was still on God's "refrigerator"!

What do you see happening in this story? Jot down a few thoughts to answer each question.

>> Why do you think Jesus helped the disciples catch fish that morning?

....

....

>> If you were Peter, what would you would have done when you realized that Jesus was on the shore?

....

....

>> How was Jesus' response different from what Peter may have expected Him to say?

....

....

....

>> Based on what Jesus said to Peter, what does Jesus think of you when you mess up?

....

....

....

>> How has God shown you His love in light of the times you have messed up?

....

....

....

....

Discover More of the Story

Just before going to the cross, Jesus told His disciples, ³⁴*A new commandment I give to you, that you love one another: just as I have loved you, you also are to love one another. ³⁵By this all people will know that you are my disciples, if you have love for one another* (John 13:34-35).

>> Clearly, one of the best ways to love God is to love others. Why do you think God feels loved when you love others?

....

....

....

Jesus replied: Love the Lord your God with all your heart and with all your soul and with all your mind. (Matthew 22:37, NIV)

>> God gives us a high challenge and asks for high commitment—that we love Him above all others and with our whole lives. What do you think it looks like to love God with all your heart, soul, and mind?

....

....

....

We love [God] because he first loved us. (1 John 4:19)

>> Your love for God grows out of His love for you. Why is it important that God loved you before you loved Him?

....

....

For this is the love of God, that we keep his command-ments. And his commandments are not burdensome. (1 John 5:3)

>> Name two or three of God's commandments (Exodus 20:1-17).

....

....

....

>> Why are God's commandments not burdensome?

....

....

....

....

The Bible says a lot about how much God loves us and how to love Him. You may want to check out these other passages.

[Jesus said] If you love me you will keep my commandments. (John 14:15)

[38]For I am sure that neither death nor life, nor angels nor rulers, nor things present nor things to come, nor powers, [39]nor height nor depth . . . will be able to separate us from the love of God in Christ Jesus our Lord. (Romans 8:38-39)

By this we know love, that he laid down his life for us, and we ought to lay down our lives for the brothers. (1 John 3:16)

Little children, let us not love in word or talk but in deed and in truth. (1 John 3:18)

My Story

I stood behind home plate on my school softball field. It was a familiar place. I could almost hear my name announced: "Now batting, centerfielder Justine Lewis." Tonight it felt strange being there alone in the dark. My team wasn't there, and the bleachers sat empty in the moonlight.

I needed to get away. My feet didn't stop until I had walked the mile from my house to home plate. I was mad at God.

It all had started three months earlier. My brother's girlfriend, who had become a good friend of mine, was involved in a terrible car accident that left her in a coma, and I was devastated. The last three months had been filled with hard days. Much of the time my parents were with my brother who lived two hours away. I was in tenth grade, and my sister was a freshman in college, so we were left at home to continue with school. My brother was one of my closest friends, and it was so painful to watch him suffer.

Day in and day out I asked Jesus to heal Lisa's injuries and my brother's heart. It seemed that the God I had so faithfully loved since I was seven years old was not listening. With each step I grew angrier. My life was in chaos, and my heart was broken. I was not sure God loved me anymore, and I certainly didn't love Him.

Completely empty, I was too exhausted to even cry. The rage spilled out, and I yelled at God, "All these years I have loved You and followed You, but I don't need You anymore. I don't trust You."

Slowly I sat down on home plate as I finished yelling at God. After a few moments the same questions Jesus asked of Peter came to mind. I had heard them recently in a sermon at church.

"Do you love Me?" I couldn't get it out of my mind.

"Do you love Me?" Why did I keep hearing that?

"Do you love Me?" Was God asking me if I loved Him?

Finally I replied, "I don't know how to love You anymore." The words frightened me as they came out of my mouth. Could I really tell God I didn't love or trust Him? Somehow I knew I was letting God down, and yet I couldn't help it. Half expecting lightning to strike me, I sat for a moment and waited.

Somewhere in my heart and my head, I felt God saying to me, "Justine, can I show you My love again and help you to love Me too?"

I pondered that thought for a few moments. Could I learn to love God again? Could I accept His love for me?

Life didn't suddenly become perfect after that encounter with God. My brother's girlfriend never fully recovered. She spent four months in a coma and a year in a rehabilitation hospital. Many years later she still suffers the effects of brain damage. It was quite a while before my brother was able to move on, and our family, as well as Lisa's, has never been the same. However, that night on the softball field as a tenth grade high school student, I made a decision to trust God and learn to love Him again. I have never regretted that choice. God forgave me for not trusting Him and for yelling at Him. In return He shows me every day how much He loves me.

Some days loving God is easy, and some days I have to depend on His help to love Him. Even on the days I don't feel or see His love, He is still faithful.

The amazing part is that the more I allow God to show me how to love Him, the more I actually love Him, and the more I feel His love for me.

So, how do I love God? Every morning I choose to:

>> Remember how deeply God loves me.
>> Ask God to show me how to love Him that day. (He shows me through prayer and His Word.)
>> Look for opportunities to love the people He brings into my life.
>> Remain confident of God's forgiveness.

The journey has had its ups and downs, but God has never removed my picture from His "refrigerator"!

Our Story

Church is an excellent place to learn more about loving God. Community gives us the most opportunities to live out our love for God and discover more of the ways our stories connect to God's Story. Studying the Bible and singing worship songs together are all great ways to love God, as are praying with, learning from, and serving others.

We are adopted into God's family when we surrender to Jesus.

3Praise be to the God and Father of our Lord Jesus Christ, who has blessed us in the heavenly realms with every spiritual blessing in Christ. 4For he chose us in him before the creation of the world to be holy and blameless in his sight. In love 5he predestined us to be adopted as his sons through Jesus Christ, in accordance with his pleasure and will. (Ephesians 1:3-5, NIV)

Because of God's love we are adopted and become part of His family of followers. This is another reason why the church community is so important in your life. This is your adopted family. That moment of surrender to God is when He adopts us. Can you imagine Him hanging your picture on His "fridge"?

In community with others who love Jesus—that is where we get nourished and stretched and held accountable so we can go out into the world and love God by loving others.

Remember Jesus' words after Peter said he loved Him? "Feed My sheep." Jesus was telling Peter that if he really loved God, he had to be willing to serve and care for others.

Sheep feeding happens best with other Christians with whom you are learning. Church is a key place where God teaches us how to love Him and how to know and understand His love for us.

The Story Continues

Imagine God is asking you, "Do you love Me?" Take a moment and ponder this question. Then write a prayer in the space in the next column, and tell God if you love Him and why or why not. Be honest. If you are having trouble loving Him right now, tell Him why. If your love for Him is overflowing right now, tell Him why. Look back on this prayer regularly. It will be a comfort in times of struggle and a reminder of how far you have come in learning to love God.

God: "Do you love Me, ...? (write your name here)

Dear God,

Want to know how to love God? Start at the source. God loves you and gives you the ability to love Him and others. Ask God every day to show you how to love Him more.

Here are a few ideas to get you started (there are many, many more).

>> Help your neighbor with a project.
>> Call a friend, and tell that person what you appreciate about him or her.
>> Sing some worship songs to Jesus.
>> Every day write down one thing you saw Jesus do in your life.
>> Pray for someone who doesn't yet know Jesus.
>> Help someone in your family without being asked.
>> Use one of your talents to bring glory to God.
>> Sit outside and observe the incredible beauty of God's creation.
>> Share God's Story with one of your friends who doesn't know Jesus.
>> Tell someone what God is teaching you.

Choose two ways to love God from the list above and write them here.

....

....

Now think of one other way (not from the list—make up your own) that you will show God your love for Him this week and write it here.

....

Here's one more idea to help you learn to love God more. Don't freak out when you feel angry with Him. Talk to Him, and tell Him how you feel. Ask Him to help you resolve the anger. Right now finish this sentence: I felt angry with God when . . .

....

After writing down these love-actions, ask God to help you love Him this week. Remember, your love is an outpouring of His great love for you. As you work on loving God this week, why not ask one of your friends to pray for you too?

Here is your chance to put God on *your* "refrigerator"! Copy the four main Scripture verses from the "Discover More of the Story" section onto note cards. Stick them on your refrigerator or anyplace you are sure to see them every day. It isn't God's picture, but it will help you keep Him front and center in your life.

{ **CHAPTER 6**

How Can I Learn to Love People?

PUTTING GOD'S LOVE INTO ACTION

Complete the following sentences.

>> In three to five words, I would describe *real* love as . . .

....

>> Love is difficult because . . .

....

>> I feel unable to love others when . . .

....

>> The person most difficult for me to love is ....

...................................., because . . . .

....

>> My favorite movie love story is ....,

because . . . .

Story Time

>> Tell a short story or draw a picture to remember a time when you felt extremely loved or when someone went out of their way to love you.

God's Story

In this passage . . .

>> A Jewish lawyer (a religion scholar) tested Jesus' knowledge by asking Him questions, to see if He really knew what He was talking about.

>> Jesus told a story to show the lawyer that following God involves much more than just knowing all the right facts.

Pay attention to what Jesus' story says about how to live, love God, and love others.

[25]*And behold, a lawyer stood up to put him to the test, saying, "Teacher, what shall I do to inherit eternal life?"*

[26]*He said to him, "What is written in the Law? How do you read it?"*

[27]*And he answered, "You shall love the Lord your God with all your heart and with all your soul and with all your strength and with all your mind, and your neighbor as yourself."*

[28]*And he said to him, "You have answered correctly; do this, and you will live."*

[29]*But he, desiring to justify himself, said to Jesus, "And who is my neighbor?"*

[30]*Jesus replied, "A man was going down from Jerusalem to Jericho, and he fell among robbers, who stripped him and beat him and departed, leaving him half dead. [31]Now by chance a priest was going down that road, and when he saw him he passed by on the other side. [32]So likewise a Levite, when he came to the place and saw him, passed by on the other side. [33]But a Samaritan, as he journeyed, came to where he was, and when he saw him, he had compassion. [34]He went to him and bound up his wounds, pouring on oil and wine. Then he set him on his own animal and brought him to an inn and took care of him. [35]And the next day he took out two denarii [two day's wages] and gave them to the innkeeper, saying, 'Take care of him, and whatever more you spend, I will repay you when I come back.'*

[36]*"Which of these three, do you think, proved to be a neighbor to the man who fell among the robbers?"*

[37]*He said, "The one who showed him mercy."*

And Jesus said to him, "You go, and do likewise." (Luke 10:25-37)

Investigate the Story

This section will help you understand the above passage and how it relates to your life. Work through this section, answering the questions in the space provided.

At the beginning of this passage, Jesus asked the lawyer to describe what he thought it meant to follow God. The lawyer answered correctly, but Jesus went a step further and told the lawyer to "go" and "do" these things. These are action words! Having the facts is not enough; we actually have to live it! Our actions show proof of our faith.

As an expert in law, this man wanted all the details figured out. He asked Jesus to clarify things. Who exactly was his neighbor? In this context, "neighbor" refers to other people with whom you come in contact, whether you know them or not. To answer the question, Jesus told a story about a man who was robbed, severely beaten, and left on the road for dead.

>> Who walked past the injured man first? Why is his reaction surprising?

....

....

>> Why do you think he reacted that way? What might have been going through his mind?

....

....

The second man to walk by was a Levite. The Levites were a tribe of people set apart for service in the Lord's Temple as priests, assistants to priests, etc. Sadly, this man's reaction was the same as the first priest.

>> Tell a short story or draw a picture about a time you ignored someone who needed help. Why did you react this way?

The next man to walk by was a Samaritan. Quick history lesson: The Samaritans were a group of people despised by the Jews. Because of their race and beliefs, Jews saw them as inferior. Jews even would go way out of their way to avoid passing through the land of Samaria.

>> Why do you think Jesus used a Samaritan as the hero of the story? What point was He trying to make?

....

....

>> What fears or hesitations might the Samaritan have had to over-come to stop and help the injured man?

....

....

>> What sacrifices did the Samaritan make to help the injured man?

....

....

Jesus finished the story by saying that the Samaritan "proved" to be a good neighbor to the man. Truly loving our neighbors requires taking action and sacrificing our own comfort and convenience for the good of others. It requires showing compassion to those we meet, even when the situation is difficult or the person is hard to love!

>> In light of this story, what do you think it means to love your neighbor "as yourself"?

....

....

>> What holds you back from loving people this way? What do you think God wants you to do about it?

....

>> Who are your neighbors? Think about different individuals or groups of people you are around regularly or may have recently met.

....

....

>> Take a moment to ask God which neighbors He may want you to reach out to and show love to (family members, friends, acquaintances, teachers, almost-strangers, coaches, teammates, etc.). Jot their names down.

....

....

Keep these people in mind as you work through the remaining sections of this chapter.

Discover More of the Story

Here are some verses to get you thinking about loving others.

Read the verses and explanations, and then answer the questions.

43 "You have heard that it was said, 'You shall love your neighbor and hate your enemy.' 44 But I say to you, Love your enemies and pray for those who persecute you, 45 so that you may be sons of your Father who is in heaven. . . . 46 For if you love those who love you, what reward do you have? Do not even the tax collectors do the same? 47 And if you greet only your brothers, what more are you doing than others? Do not even the Gentiles do the same? 48 You therefore must be perfect, as your heavenly Father is perfect." (Matthew 5:43-48)

This verse says that God calls us to go beyond loving only our own friends. Even people who don't know God do that! It's definitely easier to avoid loving difficult people, but God asks us to love them anyway, just like He loves us despite our imperfections!

>> Think about the people you listed at the end of the previous section. Which of these people are difficult for you to love? Why?

....

....

>> Whether a person is easy or hard for you to love, how could learning his or her life story help you understand him or her better and love him or her better?

....

....

¹Therefore be imitators of God, as beloved children. ²And walk in love, as Christ loved us and gave himself up for us, a fragrant offering and sacrifice to God. (Ephesians 5:1-2)

Because of the way Jesus loves us, we are able to love others. Take note: true love requires sacrifice. It's not about gaining something in return, but rather putting yourself aside and serving others. It's really about God. We do it as an act of worship unto Him.

>> In what ways does this verse change your perspective on loving the people on your list?

....

....

>> What sacrifices might you have to make to love the people you listed?

....

....

⁹Let love be genuine. Abhor what is evil; hold fast to what is good. ¹⁰Love one another with brotherly affection. Outdo one another in showing honor. . . . ¹⁴Bless those who persecute you; bless and do not curse them. ¹⁵Rejoice with those who rejoice, weep with those who weep. ¹⁶Live in harmony with one another. Do not be haughty, but associate with the lowly. Never be wise in your own sight. ¹⁷Repay no one evil for evil, but give thought to do what is honorable in the sight of all. ¹⁸If possible, so far as it depends on you, live peaceably with all. ¹⁹Beloved, never avenge yourselves, but leave it to the wrath of God, for it is written, "Vengeance is mine, I will repay, says the Lord." ²⁰To the contrary, "if your enemy is hungry, feed him; if he is thirsty, give him something to drink; for by so doing you will heap burning coals on his head." ²¹Do not be overcome by evil, but overcome evil with good. (Romans 12:9-10, 14-21)

The Jewish lawyer was right when he said that the two most important things in life are to love God with all our heart, soul, strength, and mind and to love our neighbors as ourselves. Other verses say that God's love is fully expressed and complete when we pass it on. Romans 12 describes what it looks like to practically love others in day-to-day living.

>> Why is experiencing God's love and loving Him back with all your heart, soul, strength, and mind necessary before you are able to love your neighbor as yourself?

....

....

....

>> This passage gives us a list of important ways we can love others. Write down the ones you most need to work on. Think about how you can go about doing them.

....

....

....

My Story

My name is Cassie. The beginning of this school year was hard for me. I'm a junior, but most of my friends graduated last year. I felt so alone. At lunch, I would just wander around school or eat alone in my car.

One day I met a girl named Madison. She invited me to eat lunch with her and her group of friends. Problem was, the girls she ate with not only were sophomores, but they also partied a lot. I wasn't sure I wanted to spend my lunch with them.

Then I realized something; these girls were exactly who God wanted me to eat lunch with! My days belong to Jesus, and I need to be more willing to go out of my way to love people the way He loves me. So, I began to eat lunch with Madison and her friends.

Soon I noticed that Madison was the outcast of the group. The other girls usually ignored her. I got to know Madison and hung out with her more often. God wants us to love people, so I knew that I needed to accept Madison for who she is, unlike her other "friends."

The more time I spent with Madison, the more I understood why the other girls were ignoring her. She's very clingy. If I go somewhere else for lunch, she calls me wondering where I am and is upset that I'm not there. When my friends came home from college for Christmas break, Madison felt betrayed that I spent time with them instead of her.

These things helped me realize that Madison is probably afraid of being abandoned. She is afraid of people walking out of her life and forgetting about her. Maybe something bad happened to her that makes her feel this way. Despite how difficult and annoying she can be, I know that God wants me to continue to love Madison and to be her friend. I'm trying my best. I have invited her to church with me, brought dinner to her and her family, helped her with her homework, and other stuff.

God is using Madison to teach me how to truly love people, even those who are difficult to love. God is challenging me to go out of my way to love people the way He loves me.

One day during lunch, as Madison and I were walking around school, I noticed a freshman boy sitting alone. I told Madison she was welcome to keep walking, but I was going to go sit with him and talk with him. Madison replied in shock, "Do you really do things like that?" I said, "Well, I try to." Madison said she wanted to come along.

The kid was pretty quiet when I talked with him. But after we walked away, Madison looked at me and said, "Cassie, can we do that all the time?"

God is cool. Not only is He teaching me how to love Him and love others, but He's also using what I'm learning to help Madison learn about God and loving others.

It's really true. Life really *is* all about loving God and loving others. Hopefully I can keep getting better at both. I have a lot to learn, but He is patient with me!

Our Story

Work through the following section, which discusses the importance of being in community with other believers.

> [24]*And let us consider how to stir up one another to love and good works,* [25]*not neglecting to meet together, as is the habit of some, but encouraging one another, and all the more as you see the Day drawing near. (Hebrews 10:24-25)*

The word *community* refers to a unified group of individuals who share something in common. In our case, we have Christ in common, and we are His Body—the Church.

>> Based on what you've learned so far about loving people, why do you think God wants us to be in community?

....

....

>> In the space below, write out a short story or draw a picture about a time you experienced true community. What made it feel like true community? What did you learn from the experience?

>> In what ways does true community make you feel loved? How does it help you learn to love others?

....

....

Community—the good, the bad, and the ugly.

Community is where we learn to love people. It's where we learn to be committed to people, to be real with people, to communicate well, to know others and to be known, to find help and give help, and to serve and be served. Community means we *do life* with people, together experiencing the ups and downs, the in-betweens, the easy and hard times, and the agreements and disagreements. When we continue to love each other through all of those things, deeper relationship will result. Community reminds us that this world does not revolve around us. It reminds us of Jesus' sacrifice and His love for us. And lastly, but very importantly, it reminds us that we were created to be together. We *need* to be together.

Jesus tells us to be in community both with people who are like us (this part is easy) and with those who are not like us (this part is not so easy). Remember Matthew 5:43-48? Jesus specifically asks us to go beyond what's easy and to love those who take more effort. And here's the kicker: loving someone means pursuing that person the way Jesus pursues us. Seek out the person rather than waiting for him or her to come to you!

>> Think again about the people you included on your list earlier. How can Christians in your community help you take steps to pursue and love those people better?

....

....

Take a moment to look at what Jesus has to say about all of this:

I in them and you in me, that they may become perfectly one, so that the world may know that you sent me and loved them even as you loved me. (John 17:23)

By this all people will know that you are my disciples, if you have love for one another. (John 13:35)

>> What does Jesus say will lead to the world knowing Him and His love? Yes, that's right: love and unity. This is the only recipe the Bible gives us. If we display love and unity, the world will see God's love in us and come to know Him.

Powerful, isn't it? This is the Church's mission in the world—to love God first and to love others. Then the whole world will know His love!

The Story Continues

The following section will help you take everything you've learned in this chapter and make it practical for your day-to-day life.

Loving people involves much more than sending mushy feelings in someone's general direction. Love means action. It means reaching out to people who have been overlooked by others. It means serving people and meeting needs. Love can look a million different ways because of the many different needs people have. Think back to the example in Cassie's story.

We've talked a lot about what it means to love other people. Now it's time to *go* and *do* it—just like

Jesus told the Jewish lawyer in the story about the Good Samaritan.

Here's a chart to help you do just that. Follow the instructions to fill it out.

Column 1: Remember the names you wrote down earlier (page 74)? The people God's calling you to love? Write their names in the Name column. You can also add any new names you've thought of along the way.

Column 2: To the right of each name, write down a few of the needs you see in their lives. What seems to be going on in their hearts? These can be physical, emotional, or spiritual needs. (Example: Cassie thought she saw that Madison was afraid of abandonment.) If you don't know their stories well enough to know their needs, use this column to write down some practical ways you can get to know their stories. (For example, you could invite them to hang out so you can get to know them and talk with them; you could sit next to them on the bus, in class, or at lunch; etc.)

Column 3: In this column, write down one way that you will show love and reach out to each person *this week*! Try to come up with something that meets at least one of the needs you see in each person, if you know what those needs are. (For example, you could write an encouraging note; you could ask them how they're *really* doing and *listen* to their answers; you could sit with them at lunch, invite them to coffee, invite them to hang out with your friends, offer them a ride, bring them their favorite snack when they're stressed out from studying, invite them to hang out with your family, remember their birthday; etc.) Also, one of the best ways to love your neighbors is to pray for them!

Now that you've thought of some ideas, you need to find someone to encourage you to carry them out! (Community!) Here are more instructions and a chart to get you started.

Step 1: Think of one friend (or a small group of friends) who can partner with you in loving people. This should be an individual (or individuals) who will ask you how it's going, pray with you, and help you stay committed to the people God is asking you to love. You will do the same for him or her or them.

Step 2: Call the person (people) if he or she is not sitting next to you right now. Ask this person to partner with you. Are you doing it? Seriously—pick up the phone!

Name	Needs you see in their lives or ways to discover their stories	How will you show them love *this week*?

Step 3: If the person says yes, write his or her name, phone number, and e-mail address in the chart below. If your friend says no, think of someone else and try again.

Step 4: Decide a time and place that the two of you will meet regularly to pray, encourage each other, and share stories of what God's doing. Write that information in the last column of the chart.

You're all set! Do you feel ready to go out and love God by loving others? Hopefully so! Let's close with prayer.

Jesus, please remind us of the many ways You love and pursue us. May our hearts be changed so that we desire to love You with everything in us and then pursue others, loving them the way You love us, so they may also know Your love! Amen!

Friend's Name	E-mail Address	Phone Number	Meeting Day/Time

{ **CHAPTER 7**

How Can I Learn to Listen to God?

HEARING GOD'S VOICE IN MY EVERYDAY LIFE

Everybody thinks of changing humanity and nobody thinks of changing himself.

Leo Tolstoy, *Encyclopedia of Religious Quotations*, Frank S. Mead, editor, 1965

List below all the noise in your life—for example, your iPod, your TV, your little brother, your computer, etc. Go ahead. Make a long list of everything in your life that makes a sound.

Next, circle the ten that mean the most to you.

Now number the ones you circled in order of importance for you, creating your own "top ten list of noisemakers" in your life. (Order your list from ten up to one. In other words, #1 should be your most important.)

God's Story

Before reading Luke 6:6-13, think about this: After healing a man's withered, distorted, possibly unusable arm, and before choosing His twelve leaders, Jesus . . .

>> spent the entire night alone in the desert hills, praying.
>> pulled away from His work and His friends in order to listen carefully to God.
>> knew that closeness with God happens, in part, when we stop the busy activities of life and listen.
>> rested in His Father's presence.
>> waited expectantly for instructions, guidance, encouragement, love, and joy.

Now read the story aloud.

6On another Sabbath, he entered the synagogue and was teaching, and a man was there whose right hand was withered. 7And the scribes and Pharisees watched him, to see whether he would heal on the Sabbath, so that they might find a reason to accuse him. 8But he knew their thoughts, and he said to the man with the withered hand, "Come and stand here." And he rose and stood there. 9And Jesus said to them, "I ask you, is it lawful on the Sabbath to do good or to do harm, to save life or to destroy it?" 10And after looking around at them all he said to him, "Stretch out your hand." And he did so, and his hand was restored. 11But they were filled with fury and discussed with one another what they might do to Jesus. 12In these days he went out to the mountain to pray, and all night he continued in prayer to God. 13And when day came, he called his disciples and chose from them twelve, whom he named apostles. (Luke 6:6-13)

Investigate the Story

Read the following God's Story descriptions, and answer the questions. Then discuss your answers with some friends.

>> List the names of all the people (including groups of people) involved in this story (verses 6-7). Next to their names, write a brief description of each person's (or group's) reactions, attitude, and feelings about Jesus (verses 6-13).

the ....

the ....

the ....

the ....

the ....

>> Why do you think the religious people wanted to accuse Jesus? (verses 7, 11)?

....

....

....

>> During Jesus' lifetime, healing a sick person on the Sabbath (the weekly religious holy day) was illegal. This was one of many religious rules that Jesus challenged. Compassion, love, and faithfulness to God were more important to Jesus than following regulations. Jesus asked the scribes and the Pharisees (the religious people of Jesus' day) a question (verse 9). Then He waited for their answer, which never came. Read verse 9 again. Why do you suppose they did not answer Him? What might they have been thinking?

....

....

....

In the middle of two important events in the life of Jesus—healing this man (verses 6-11) and then choosing His disciples (verse 13)—Jesus pulled away and went to the mountain to pray to God—all night long! He listened to God, His Father, and talked with Him.

>> Why do you think Jesus spent so much time alone, praying?

....

....

....

>> What did Jesus need from His Father?

....

....

....

>> What do you imagine God the Father might have said to His Son, Jesus?

....

....

....

Discover More of the Story

Check out this story from the Old Testament:

⁹There he came to a cave and lodged in it. And behold, the word of the LORD came to him, and he said to him, "What are you doing here, Elijah?" ¹⁰He said, "I have been very jealous for the LORD, the God of hosts. For the people of Israel have forsaken your covenant, thrown down your altars, and killed your prophets with the sword, and I, even I only, am left, and they seek my life, to take it away." ¹¹And he said, "Go out and stand on the mount before the LORD." And behold, the LORD passed by, and a great and strong wind tore the mountains and broke in pieces the rocks before the LORD, but the LORD was not

in the wind. And after the wind an earthquake, but the LORD was not in the earthquake. ¹²And after the earthquake a fire, but the LORD was not in the fire. And after the fire the sound of a low whisper. ¹³And when Elijah heard it, he wrapped his face in his cloak and went out and stood at the entrance of the cave. And behold, there came a voice to him and said, "What are you doing here, Elijah?" ¹⁴He said, "I have been very jealous for the LORD, the God of hosts. For the people of Israel have forsaken your covenant, thrown down your altars, and killed your prophets with the sword, and I, even I only, am left, and they seek my life, to take it away." ¹⁵And the LORD said to him, "Go, return on your way to the wilderness of Damascus. . . ." (1 Kings 19:9-15)

We can all learn to discern God's "low whisper." In this story, God gave specific instructions to Elijah. They had a conversation together about what Elijah should do next. God did not speak in the great strong wind. He did not speak in the earthquake. He did not speak in the fire. He waited to speak in the "low whisper," a still, small voice. We can hear best from God when we're quiet.

>> Today take five minutes to be quiet and listen to God. Record below what you experienced. (If you can do it right now, go for it!)

....

....

....

Read this passage, also from the Old Testament.

As a deer pants for flowing streams,
so my soul pants for you, O God. My soul thirsts for God,
for the living God. When shall I come and appear
before God? . . .
By day the LORD *commands his steadfast love,*
and at night his song is with me,
a prayer to the God of my life. (Psalm 42:1-2, 8)

>> The writer of this great passage was very motivated to spend time alone with God in quietness and rest. What motivates you to spend time alone with God?

....

....

....

>> What hinders you from spending time alone with God?

....

....

....

Read one more verse about listening to God: *Now when Jesus heard this, he withdrew from there in a boat to a desolate place by himself. But when the crowds heard it, they followed him on foot from the towns* (Matthew 14:13).

Jesus had just received the news about his cousin John the Baptist's death. He withdrew by boat privately to a solitary place. John had been beheaded by Herod, an evil government ruler. In the midst of a busy ministry and this sad experience, Jesus decided to go away to a lonely place. He made going off by Himself to pray and wait on God a normal habit.

>> When in your daily life would be the best time to make a habit of quiet, restful time alone with God? (circle the two best options for you)

Early in the morning

Before work

During lunchtime

After work

Right after school

Right before dinner

Right after dinner

Late at night while everyone else is sleeping

>> What stressful or sad times have you experienced lately?

....

....

....

>> During those times, did you get alone with God? Describe how you connected with Him or what made your attempt to get together with Him difficult.

....

....

....

>> What can you learn from Jesus' example in Matthew 14:13?

....

....

....

My Story
By Deron, Sixteen

Of all the people in my life, the members of my family are the most difficult to love. Don't get me wrong: they're pretty good people. They aren't abusive or mean or stupid. But the truth is, they are my family, and loving them can be challenging. Sometimes I give up; I stop trying to love them, even though I know Jesus wants me to extend love and acceptance to them. Recently God began to talk to me about my failing attempts to love my family. On this subject, I honestly heard His voice. In John 10:3 Jesus refers to Himself when He says, *"The sheep hear his voice, and he calls his own sheep by name and leads them out."*

Making room in the busyness of life was the challenge. I learned to make room for Him by slowing down the pace of my life, just enough to become aware that He really wants to talk to me. He wants me to hear His voice and follow Him.

Not exactly audible, Jesus' voice still came through loud and clear to me in a dramatic way. (He doesn't have laryngitis! But sometimes I can't hear Him.)

The impression He left with me took my breath away. Jesus seemed to be reminding me that loving people, in general, is something He's already teaching me to do. I could almost hear Him complimenting me: "You are learning how to love people. Your love for your friends and coworkers is thriving. You even love strangers well. I was so proud of you last fall when you and your friend stopped to help that lost stranger on the street corner downtown, the man who didn't speak English and couldn't find his way. When you both went back, after the conversation ended, and offered him money for dinner, you pleased Me. And I want you to learn to love your family too. I can help. I will guide you."

Later it seemed clear that Jesus was offering me simple instructions. Trying to follow His voice, I began to make specific, intentional attempts to love my family members in the same way that I love other people. I started to ask my family members more questions and then listen to their answers—just as I try to do with my friends. I also began to pray more for my family members—the way I pray for strangers.

The amazing part of my story is that God really is helping me love my family more authentically. Sure, I'm still impatient, and they still drive me crazy sometimes, but recently we experienced some real progress. It was time for the "yearly family photograph," usually an unbearable, unpleasant, nasty family event. Determined to take a baby step toward loving my family better, I tried to turn the annual picture-taking episode into a fun family affair. My positive attitude didn't fix all the problems, but my sister-in-law and older brother noticed the change in my outlook. They were grateful. Their gratitude encouraged my younger brother. The change in his mind-set impacted my parents' view, in part because they were shocked at the transformation in my brother!

> *God spoke to me.*
> *I listened.*
> *He gently guided my actions.*
> *I listened to Him again and obeyed.*
> *He worked a small miracle in me and in my family.*

It's cool that my family actually gave credit to my younger brother for this turnaround. Jesus was pleased with this too. Jesus humbled me, and I let Him. I honestly didn't need the recognition because it's about God, not about me! My brother felt like he made this positive adjustment happen in our family. In the end he seemed encouraged, and I had the privilege of loving my family, especially my little brother.

In the entire crowded universe there is but one stupendous word: Love. (author unknown)

Our Story

Finding your place in a local church will help you listen to God. Your listening ear will be more in tune with the voice of God when you're connected to the Body of Christ. (The Bible often refers to the Church as the "Body of Christ" because the Church is designed to function like a body, Christ's Body. In perfect rhythm, connected to Christ, all Christians have a place to belong in God's Family, the Church, His Body.) Here's how to find your place in the Church.

>> List below or describe four to six Christian churches near your house.

....

....

....

....

....

>> Place a star next to the churches (if any) that you've visited.

>> Circle the churches that any of your friends attend.

>> Which one would you be willing to visit if you don't already have a church home?

Before you visit a church, think through your reasons for going. If you go to church to listen to God, to hear His voice, you set yourself up for a better experience. If you go to connect with God, it doesn't matter how good the music sounds, how much you like the pastor, or how exciting the programs are. Take your best—your "A-game"—to the church service and expect (trust) God to speak to you.

After your first visit to a church, try the following three activities:

>> Write about your experience below.

....

....

....

....

....

....

>> Go to the church's web site, and look for interesting ways you could get involved.

>> Call the youth pastor or the pastor, and ask how you could help or serve or be involved.

The Story Continues

Listening is the great story connector. It can be as easy as blogging. Here's where you get to practice hearing God's voice! As you practice, you will find yourself growing closer to God. You will have the opportunity to develop three spiritual habits over the course of the next seventeen days. When the two and a half weeks end, try to continue practicing these spiritual habits. Begin by developing prayer habits for five days, followed by habits of silence for four days, and concluding with Scripture study habits for eight days.

Prayer Instructions: Take five days to practice the spiritual habit of prayer. Follow the simple guidelines for each day. Keep a journal, a paper blog, in the space provided. Try it one day at a time, one spiritual habit at a time. Talk to your friends about how this kind of blogging is going for you.

SPIRITUAL HABIT #1: PRAYER—DAY ONE

Prayer is listening to and talking with God.

> There is nothing that makes us love people so much as praying for them. (William Law)

Today's Date: ....

>> List five people you know who would benefit from God's work in their lives.

....

....

....

....

....

>> Next to their names write out a short, confidential prayer to God on their behalves.

>> Pause in between each prayer.

>> Ask God to help you know what to ask for.

>> Listen for God's still, small voice.

>> Wait.

>> Return to the list, and write another prayer for each person, next to each of their names.

Prayer is listening. (Richard Foster)

PRAYER—DAY TWO

Today's Date: ....

Listening to the Lord is the first thing, the second thing, and the third thing necessary for prayer to be effective. (author unknown)

>> Ask God to guide your spiritual habit of prayer today.

>> Ask Him to speak to you.

>> Ask Him to help you hear His voice.

>> Tell Him what you know is true about Him.

>> Begin by writing out something short, like, "Jesus, help me to pray. I want to listen to You and talk to You. Help me hear Your voice. I'm grateful that You died on the cross for me."

....

....

....

....

....

....

>> Spend the next few minutes writing down a few words of worship to God (three to five sentences would be great). To worship God is to see Him as worthy, to attribute the greatest worth to Him, and to express to Him the reasons you want to worship Him. You

can begin by saying something like, "God, I love You. Thank You for loving me first, so completely and so unconditionally."

....

....

....

....

....

....

>> You can continue by writing something similar to Revelation 4:11: *Worthy are you, our Lord and God, to receive glory and honor and power, for you created all things, and by your will they existed and were created.*

....

....

....

....

....

PRAYER—DAY THREE

Today's Date: ....

Develop an "attitude of gratitude." (author unknown)

>> Spend today practicing the spiritual habit of prayer by being thankful to God for all that He is doing in your life. Thanksgiving is appreciation for the goodness God shows to us.

>> Spend the next few minutes writing down a few words of thanksgiving to God. You can begin by saying something like, "God, thank You for taking care of me today. Thank You for hearing my prayers about my sister. Thank You for what You did for me in algebra class. Thank You for giving me hope about next week's game." Write three to five sentences expressing your own words of gratitude to Him.

....

....

....

....

....

God often speaks to us through the words of the Bible. In 1 Thessalonians 5:16-18 God tells us about prayer and thanksgiving. He uses one sentence with three simple phrases to encourage us to pray. He also explains how we are to pray.

> [16]Rejoice always,
> [17]pray without ceasing,
> [18]give thanks in all circumstances; for this is the will of God in Christ Jesus for you.

>> Make a quick blog-list of some specifics from your life that you are grateful for today.

....

....

....

....

....

When you pray do not try to express yourself in fancy words, for it is often the simple, repetitive phrases of a little child that our Father in Heaven finds irresistible. (John Climacus)

PRAYER—DAY FOUR

Today's Date: ....

Problems arise that get in the way of our ability to hear God's voice. Sometimes we're too busy, moving too fast. Other times we can be distracted away from God by people, school, or any number of positive or negative influences. At other times our own sin sidetracks our attention away from God. The Bible is clear about how to deal with the diversion of sin. God requires us to confess our sins and turn away from whatever influences pull us away from hearing His voice.

To "confess" our sins to God simply means that we agree with God that we have offended Him, that we have hurt Him.

We humans can offend God by our actions. We can also offend God by neglecting to do something we know He wanted us to do.

To "repent" of our sins means we turn away from them. We move 180 degrees away from our sins and start moving back to God.

Jesus' friend John wrote about confession in his book 1 John (near the end of the New Testament). In 1 John 1:9 God says, *If we confess our sins, he is faithful and just to forgive us our sins and to cleanse us from all unrighteousness.*

>> List below (confidentially) some of the sins you struggled with during the last few days.

....

....

....

....

....

....

....

>> Now take the time to say the words "I'm sorry" to God. Ask for His forgiveness. Ask Him to help you hear His voice clearly as you move away from those sins. As a step of faith (a step in the right direction), read the verse again aloud: *If we confess our sins, he is faithful and just to forgive us our sins and to cleanse us from all unrighteousness* (1 John 1:9).

>> God promises to forgive our sins. You are forgiven, for sure! In your mind and in your heart, receive His promised forgiveness and love.

>> Now, as an act of trust and as a simple way to accept His love and forgiveness, put a big bold, dark line through each of the sins you listed above! Your guilt is gone!

PRAYER—DAY FIVE

Today's Date: ....

Many passages in the Bible are actually prayers. We can use them to pray to God—listening and talking to Him through His written words. Read the following prayers aloud and slowly, by yourself.

[14]For this reason I bow my knees before the Father, [15]from whom every family in heaven and on earth is named, [16]that according to the riches of his glory he may grant you to be strengthened with power through his Spirit in your inner being, [17]so that Christ may dwell in your hearts through faith—that you, being rooted and grounded in love, [18]may have strength to comprehend with all the saints what is the breadth and length and height and depth, [19]and to know the love of Christ that surpasses knowledge, that you may be filled with all the fullness of God. (Ephesians 3:14-19)

>> Underline in that passage the prayers you want to pray. For example:

that you may *be strengthened with power*

that you *may have strength to comprehend with all the saints what is the breadth and length and height and depth* of God's love

that you *may be filled with all the fullness of God*

Psalm 23 is another great source of help from God as you practice the spiritual habit of prayer. Psalms is a book of passionate, emotional, and artistic poems in the Old Testament. The writers of the psalms cry out to God in times of need, times of joy, times of sorrow, times of fear, times of hope, and times of anger. The psalm below is like a song, sung by a person who needs God to lead him or her, just as sheep would need a shepherd to protect them and lead them to safety.

>> Try praying this prayer to God aloud.

¹*The* L*ORD* *is my shepherd; I shall not want.*
²*He makes me lie down in green pastures.*
He leads me beside still waters.
³*He restores my soul.*
He leads me in paths of righteousness for his name's sake.
⁴*Even though I walk through the valley of the shadow of death,*
I will fear no evil,
for you are with me;
your rod and your staff,
they comfort me.
⁵*You prepare a table before me*
in the presence of my enemies;
you anoint my head with oil;

my cup overflows.
⁶*Surely goodness and mercy shall follow me*
all the days of my life,
and I shall dwell in the house of the L*ORD* *forever. (Psalm 23)*

Prayer is conversing, communicating with God. (Dallas Willard)

Silence Instructions: Take four days to practice the spiritual habit of silence. Follow the simple instructions for each day. Continue to keep a journal in the space provided. It's like a giant God Blog between you and Him. Try it one day at a time, one spiritual habit at a time. Talk to your friends about how this kind of blogging is going for you.

SPIRITUAL HABIT #2: SILENCE — DAY SIX

Silence is inward, uninterrupted attentiveness to God.

Today's Date: ....

One disastrous ending: Tragedy struck recently when twenty-year-old David Thorton died in a horrible car accident. He was headed westbound on Route 76 way too fast.

Exceeding 120 miles an hour, he lost control. The insane speed forced the unmanageable car to flip across three lanes of traffic into the far eastbound lane. When David's vehicle smashed into an oncoming car, both cars exploded immediately, violently killing David and the man in the other car. Life is too fragile to move that fast.

Pray this simple prayer right now: *Slow me down, Lord. I can't hear You when I move too fast. Give me a new heart and ears that hear Your voice. Help me, Jesus.*

Living life over 120 miles per hour can damage our souls. God desires that His children slow down enough to hear His voice. He wants us to listen. In order to listen, we must be still, quiet, and silent. To live a *listening life*, paying attention to God, expecting to hear His voice, we must first accept the new heart He has for us. Then we can learn to wait in silence as He speaks His words of love to us.

And I will give you a new heart, and a new spirit I will put within you. And I will remove the heart of stone from your flesh and give you a heart of flesh. (Ezekiel 36:26)

Most people's lives are either fast or deep, but doing both is impossible! To help you go deeper with God, prac-

tice the spiritual habit of silence today for ten minutes. You'll have to slow down from 120 to about 20 mph. Here's how to try it.

>> Sit comfortably alone in a room or outside.
>> Turn off and ignore everything—TV, iPod, stereo, radio, cell phone, computer, etc.
>> Ask Jesus to join you in the silence and help you to rest in Him—to wait for Him—to hear His voice.
>> Close your eyes.
>> Relax your body and acknowledge that God is here.
>> After ten minutes pass, write what you felt and thought during the silence:

....

....

....

SILENCE—DAY SEVEN

Today's Date: ....

Jesus spent a lot of time in silence, praying to God His

Father, listening, talking, and waiting. He often sought solitude in the mountains.

But [Jesus] would withdraw to desolate places and pray. (Luke 5:16)

The words of Luke stand as a commentary on the lifestyle of Jesus—a lifestyle that we also can pursue. Following the healing of the leper in Luke 5, Jesus went to a "desolate place," the wilderness, to pray.

>> Find a quiet place (your own "desolate place" or mountaintop) to pray alone. Take with you three things only—this book, your Bible, and a pen. When you have found a silent place to be alone with Jesus, blog your thoughts and then listen.

....

....

At times Jesus would invite His closest friends to come away with Him for prayer.

And he said to them, "Come away by yourselves to a desolate place and rest a while." (Mark 6:31)

Which of your friends could you invite to pray with you?...

Silence and prayer can happen alone or with friends. Try it both ways.

SILENCE—DAY EIGHT

Today's Date: ....

Life is a journey and love is what makes the journey worthwhile. (author unknown)

Kind words can be short and easy to speak, but their echoes are truly endless. (Mother Teresa)

Silent time with God helps us develop a love for the people around us.

>> Spend ten minutes in silent prayer with God. Ask Him to reveal those to whom He wants you to show love and kindness. (Remember, He's already at work in the lives of the people you love!) Wait for words from Him. Write the names down here. Spend one more minute praying for everyone on this list.

....

....

....

....

....

....

....

(To help with this activity, go back to Chapter 6, and check out the list you already created.)

Solitude and Silence teach me to love my brothers [and sisters] in the faith for what they are. (Thomas Merton)

SILENCE—DAY NINE

Today's Date: ....

"Be still, and know that I am God.
I will be exalted among the nations,
I will be exalted in the earth!" (Psalm 46:10)

>> For today, don't write anything in your *Living the Story* blog. Simply read the verse from Psalm 46:10 aloud, slowly: *"Be still, and know that I am God. I will be exalted among the nations, I will be exalted in the earth!"*
>> Think about God and all that you've learned about Him so far.
>> Read the verse again, slowly: *"Be still, and know that I am God. I will be exalted among the nations, I will be exalted in the earth!"*
>> Think about what it means to *"be still."*
>> Think about the meaning of *"know that I am God."*

>> Read the verse one last time for today: *"Be still, and know that I am God. I will be exalted among the nations, I will be exalted in the earth!"*

Silence is the safest way to God. (St. Anthony of the Desert Fathers)

Scripture Study Instructions: Take eight days to practice the spiritual habit of Scripture study. Follow the simple instructions for each day. Continue to keep a journal, a paper blog, in the space provided. Try it one day at a time, one spiritual habit at a time. Talk to your friends about how this kind of blogging is going for you.

SPIRITUAL HABIT #3:
SCRIPTURE STUDY—DAY TEN

Scripture study is engaging personally in the written Word of God.

Today's Date: ....

When we read a portion of the Bible, we want our hearts, minds, and actions to be directed by what God means in His Word. To understand what God means, we have to study His words carefully. At first this might feel difficult. While it does take practice, it will get easier! Over the next four days you will read the book of Colossians. Read it slowly, asking God to speak to you through His Word.

Today read aloud Colossians 1.

¹*Paul, an apostle of Christ Jesus by the will of God, and Timothy our brother,*

²*To the saints and faithful brothers in Christ at Colossae: Grace to you and peace from God our Father.*

³*We always thank God, the Father of our Lord Jesus Christ, when we pray for you, ⁴since we heard of your faith in Christ Jesus and of the love that you have for all the saints, ⁵because of the hope laid up for you in heaven. Of this you have heard before in the word of the truth, the gospel, ⁶which has come to you, as indeed in the whole world it is bearing fruit and growing—as it also does among you, since the day you heard it and understood the grace of God in truth, ⁷just as you learned it from Epaphras our beloved fellow servant. He is a faithful minister of Christ on your behalf ⁸and has made known to us your love in the Spirit.*

⁹*And so, from the day we heard, we have not ceased to pray for you, asking that you may be filled with the knowledge of his will in all spiritual wisdom and understanding, ¹⁰so as to walk in a manner worthy of the Lord, fully pleasing to him, bearing fruit in every good work and increasing in the knowledge of God. ¹¹May you be strengthened with all power, according to his glorious might, for all endurance and patience with joy, ¹²giving thanks to the Father, who has qualified you to share in the inheritance of the saints in light. ¹³He has delivered us from the domain of darkness and transferred us to the kingdom of his beloved Son, ¹⁴in whom we have redemption, the forgiveness of sins.*

¹⁵*He is the image of the invisible God, the firstborn of all creation. ¹⁶For by him all things were created, in heaven and on earth, visible and invisible, whether thrones or dominions or rulers or authorities—all things were created through him and for him. ¹⁷And he is before all things, and in him all things hold together. ¹⁸And he is the head of the body, the church. He is the beginning, the firstborn from the dead, that in everything he might be preeminent. ¹⁹For in him all the fullness of God was pleased to dwell, ²⁰and through him to reconcile to himself all things, whether on earth or in heaven, making peace by the blood of his cross.*

²¹*And you, who once were alienated and hostile in mind, doing evil deeds, ²²he has now reconciled in his body of flesh by his death, in order to present you holy and blameless and above reproach before him, ²³if indeed you continue in the faith, stable and steadfast, not shifting from the hope of the gospel that you heard, which has been proclaimed in all creation under heaven, and of which I, Paul, became a minister.*

²⁴*Now I rejoice in my sufferings for your sake, and in my flesh I am filling up what is lacking in Christ's afflictions for the sake of his body, that is, the church, ²⁵of which I became a minister according to the stewardship from God*

that was given to me for you, to make the word of God fully known, [26]the mystery hidden for ages and generations but now revealed to his saints. [27]To them God chose to make known how great among the Gentiles are the riches of the glory of this mystery, which is Christ in you, the hope of glory. [28]Him we proclaim, warning everyone and teaching everyone with all wisdom, that we may present everyone mature in Christ. [29]For this I toil, struggling with all his energy that he powerfully works within me.

>> Write below one important phrase or sentence from this chapter.

....

....

....

Great job. Tomorrow you'll read aloud Colossians 2.

SCRIPTURE STUDY—DAY ELEVEN

Today's Date: ....
Read aloud, slowly, Colossians 2.

[1]For I want you to know how great a struggle I have for you and for those at Laodicea and for all who have not seen me face to face, [2]that their hearts may be encouraged, being knit together in love, to reach all the riches of full assurance of understanding and the knowledge of God's mystery, which is Christ, [3]in whom are hidden all the treasures of wisdom and knowledge. [4]I say this in order that no one may delude you with plausible arguments. [5]For though I am absent in body, yet I am with you in spirit, rejoicing to see your good order and the firmness of your faith in Christ.

[6]Therefore, as you received Christ Jesus the Lord, so walk in him, [7]rooted and built up in him and established in the faith, just as you were taught, abounding in thanksgiving.

[8]See to it that no one takes you captive by philosophy and empty deceit, according to human tradition, according to the elemental spirits of the world, and not according to Christ. [9]For in him the whole fullness of deity dwells bodily, [10]and you have been filled in him, who is the head of all rule and authority. [11]In him also you were circumcised with a circumcision made without hands, by putting off the body of the flesh, by the circumcision of Christ, [12]having been buried with him in baptism, in which you were also raised with him through faith in the powerful working of God, who raised him from the dead. [13]And you, who were dead in your trespasses and the uncircumcision of your flesh, God made alive together with him, having forgiven us all our trespasses, [14]by canceling the record of debt that stood against us with its legal demands. This he set

aside, nailing it to the cross. ¹⁵*He disarmed the rulers and authorities and put them to open shame, by triumphing over them in him.*

¹⁶*Therefore let no one pass judgment on you in questions of food and drink, or with regard to a festival or a new moon or a Sabbath.* ¹⁷*These are a shadow of the things to come, but the substance belongs to Christ.* ¹⁸*Let no one disqualify you, insisting on asceticism and worship of angels, going on in detail about visions, puffed up without reason by his sensuous mind,* ¹⁹*and not holding fast to the Head, from whom the whole body, nourished and knit together through its joints and ligaments, grows with a growth that is from God.*

²⁰*If with Christ you died to the elemental spirits of the world, why, as if you were still alive in the world, do you submit to regulations—* ²¹*"Do not handle, Do not taste, Do not touch"* ²²*(referring to things that all perish as they are used)—according to human precepts and teachings?* ²³*These have indeed an appearance of wisdom in promoting self-made religion and asceticism and severity to the body, but they are of no value in stopping the indulgence of the flesh.*

>> Write below one important phrase or sentence from Colossians 2.

....

....

Nice! You are now halfway through reading the entire book of Colossians. You can continue tomorrow.

SCRIPTURE STUDY—DAY TWELVE

Today's Date: ....

Read Colossians 3 aloud, slowly. Think carefully about what you are reading.

¹*If then you have been raised with Christ, seek the things that are above, where Christ is, seated at the right hand of God.* ²*Set your minds on things that are above, not on things that are on earth.* ³*For you have died, and your life is hidden with Christ in God.* ⁴*When Christ who is your life appears, then you also will appear with him in glory.*

⁵*Put to death therefore what is earthly in you: sexual immorality, impurity, passion, evil desire, and covetousness, which is idolatry.* ⁶*On account of these the wrath of God is coming.* ⁷*In these you too once walked, when you were living in them.* ⁸*But now you must put them all away: anger, wrath, malice, slander, and obscene talk from your mouth.* ⁹*Do not lie to one another, seeing that you have put off the old self with its practices* ¹⁰*and have put on the new self, which is being renewed in knowledge after the image of its creator.* ¹¹*Here there is not Greek and Jew, circumcised and uncircumcised, barbarian, Scythian, slave, free; but Christ is all, and in all.*

¹²*Put on then, as God's chosen ones, holy and beloved, compassionate hearts, kindness, humility, meekness, and patience, ¹³bearing with one another and, if one has a complaint against another, forgiving each other; as the Lord has forgiven you, so you also must forgive. ¹⁴And above all these put on love, which binds everything together in perfect harmony. ¹⁵And let the peace of Christ rule in your hearts, to which indeed you were called in one body. And be thankful. ¹⁶Let the word of Christ dwell in you richly, teaching and admonishing one another in all wisdom, singing psalms and hymns and spiritual songs, with thankfulness in your hearts to God. ¹⁷And whatever you do, in word or deed, do everything in the name of the Lord Jesus, giving thanks to God the Father through him.*

¹⁸*Wives, submit to your husbands, as is fitting in the Lord. ¹⁹Husbands, love your wives, and do not be harsh with them. ²⁰Children, obey your parents in everything, for this pleases the Lord. ²¹Fathers, do not provoke your children, lest they become discouraged. ²²Slaves, obey in everything those who are your earthly masters, not by way of eye-service, as people-pleasers, but with sincerity of heart, fearing the Lord. ²³Whatever you do, work heartily, as for the Lord and not for men, ²⁴knowing that from the Lord you will receive the inheritance as your reward. You are serving the Lord Christ. ²⁵For the wrongdoer will be paid back for the wrong he has done, and there is no partiality.*

>> Write below one important phrase or sentence from Colossians 3.

....

....

....

Very good! Tomorrow you will finish reading the book of Colossians.

SCRIPTURE STUDY—DAY THIRTEEN

Today's Date: ....

Read aloud and slowly Colossians 4. Listen for God's voice in His Word.

¹*Masters, treat your slaves justly and fairly, knowing that you also have a Master in heaven.*

²*Continue steadfastly in prayer, being watchful in it with thanksgiving. ³At the same time, pray also for us, that God may open to us a door for the word, to declare the mystery of Christ, on account of which I am in prison— ⁴that I may make it clear, which is how I ought to speak.*

⁵*Conduct yourselves wisely toward outsiders, making the best use of the time. ⁶Let your speech always be gracious, seasoned with salt, so that you may know how you ought to answer each person.*

⁷*Tychicus will tell you all about my activities. He is a beloved brother and faithful minister and fellow servant in the Lord. ⁸I have sent him to you for this very purpose, that you may know how we are and that he may encourage your hearts, ⁹and with him Onesimus, our faithful and beloved brother, who is one of you. They will tell you of everything that has taken place here.*

¹⁰*Aristarchus my fellow prisoner greets you, and Mark the cousin of Barnabas (concerning whom you have received instructions—if he comes to you, welcome him), ¹¹and Jesus who is called Justus. These are the only men of the circumcision among my fellow workers for the kingdom of God, and they have been a comfort to me. ¹²Epaphras, who is one of you, a servant of Christ Jesus, greets you, always struggling on your behalf in his prayers, that you may stand mature and fully assured in all the will of God. ¹³For I bear him witness that he has worked hard for you and for those in Laodicea and in Hierapolis. ¹⁴Luke the beloved physician greets you, as does Demas. ¹⁵Give my greetings to the brothers at Laodicea, and to Nympha and the church in her house. ¹⁶And when this letter has been read among you, have it also read in the church of the Laodiceans; and see that you also read the letter from Laodicea. ¹⁷And say to Archippus, "See that you fulfill the ministry that you have received in the Lord."*

¹⁸*I, Paul, write this greeting with my own hand. Remember my chains. Grace be with you.*

>> Write below one important phrase or sentence from Colossians 4.

....

....

....

Great work! Congratulations. You have finished reading an entire book of the Bible. After finishing this book, continue reading the Bible regularly (try reading one chapter per day) so that you can grow closer to Christ!

SCRIPTURE STUDY—DAY FOURTEEN

Today's Date: ....

To study the Bible is to chew on the words as though they were food. God's Word can indeed be nourishment to us. Chew on this passage for a while.

¹*If I speak in the tongues of men and of angels, but have not love, I am a noisy gong or a clanging cymbal.* ²*And if I have prophetic powers, and understand all mysteries and all knowledge, and if I have all faith, so as to remove mountains, but have not love, I am nothing.* ³*If I give away all I have, and if I deliver up my body to be burned, but have not love, I gain nothing.*

⁴*Love is patient and kind; love does not envy or boast; it is not arrogant* ⁵*or rude. It does not insist on its own way; it is not irritable or resentful;* ⁶*it does not rejoice at wrongdoing, but rejoices with the truth.* ⁷*Love bears all things, believes all things, hopes all things, endures all things.*

⁸*Love never ends. As for prophecies, they will pass away; as for tongues, they will cease; as for knowledge, it will pass away.* ⁹*For we know in part and we prophesy in part,* ¹⁰*but when the perfect comes, the partial will pass away.* ¹¹*When I was a child, I spoke like a child, I thought like a child, I reasoned like a child. When I became a man, I gave up childish ways.* ¹²*For now we see in a mirror dimly, but then face to face. Now I know in part; then I shall know fully, even as I have been fully known.*

¹³*So now faith, hope, and love abide, these three; but the greatest of these is love. (1 Corinthians 13)*

>> Even though Jesus is not mentioned directly, how do you see Him in the words of this chapter?

....

....

....

....

....

....

....

....

Life is a song. Love is the music. (author unknown)

SCRIPTURE STUDY—DAY FIFTEEN

Today's Date: ....

In the Bible, God spends a lot of time teaching us about love. Check out this passage!

7Beloved, let us love one another, for love is from God, and whoever loves has been born of God and knows God. 8Anyone who does not love does not know God, because God is love. 9In this the love of God was made manifest among us, that God sent his only Son into the world, so that we might live through him. 10In this is love, not that we have loved God but that he loved us and sent his Son to be the propitiation for our sins. 11Beloved, if God so loved us, we also ought to love one another. 12No one has ever seen God; if we love one another, God abides in us and his love is perfected in us.

13By this we know that we abide in him and he in us, because he has given us of his Spirit. 14And we have seen and testify that the Father has sent his Son to be the Savior of the world. 15Whoever confesses that Jesus is the Son of God, God abides in him, and he in God. 16So we have come to know and to believe the love that God has for us. God is love, and whoever abides in love abides in God, and God abides in him. 17By this is love perfected with us, so that we may have confidence for the day of judgment, because as he is so also are we in this world. 18There is no fear in love, but perfect love casts out fear. For fear has to do with punishment, and whoever fears has not been perfected in love. 19We love because he first loved us. 20If anyone says, "I love God," and hates his brother, he is a liar; for he who does not love his brother whom he has seen cannot love God whom he has not seen. 21And this commandment we have from him: whoever loves God must also love his brother. (1 John 4:7-21)

>> Circle the word *love* each time it appears in the passage above.

>> What's one way that you could express love for Jesus Christ today?

....

....

>> What's one way that you could love someone else today?

....

....

SCRIPTURE STUDY—DAY SIXTEEN

Today's Date: ....

Prayerfully, steadily focus on this one sentence from God's Word: *For by grace you have been saved through faith. And this is not your own doing; it is the gift of God* (Ephesians 2:8).

Can you memorize it?

>> Read it aloud. Read it again, slowly.

>> Now write Ephesians 2:8 below. Refer back to your Bible or to the verse above for help.

....

....

....

>> Now cover your paper and close your Bible. Try to write Ephesians 2:8 below without any help.

....

....

....

....

>> One last thing. Say the verse aloud, reading what you wrote

above. Then turn your paper over, and say it out loud from memory.

Nice work! Practice again tomorrow.

SCRIPTURE STUDY—DAY SEVENTEEN

Today's Date: ....

>> Attend church this week, and bring this book along so you can take a few notes on what the pastor says about the Bible. Which church will you attend?

....

....

....

....

....

....

....

....

....

....

....

....

Jesus through *Living the Story?* Order a new copy of *Living the Story* (you can buy it on the Crossway Books web site—www.crossway.com), and give it as a gift to someone you love. Invite that person to join you on the adventure of *Living the Story,* connecting God's Story to your story and your story to your friend's story. You have the privilege of passing God's love onto someone else.

Wow! You made it. Celebrate the last seventeen days. You journeyed with Jesus through three spiritual habits—prayer, silence, and Scripture study. You've been practicing some of the very things Jesus practiced in order to be close to His Father and abide in His Father's love.

As you finish this important book, consider sharing God's Story with someone else. Do you have a friend or a family member who might benefit from connecting with

Celebration and Congratulations Letter

You did it!

Way to go!

You made it!

You found your way through the pages of *Living the Story.* We are confident that Jesus has loved you and changed you in the process. (He has really changed us too!) Your connection to God's Story is stronger than ever, and the journey is just beginning!

As we wrote these pages, we were praying. We didn't know all the people who would be affected by this book, but we asked Jesus to make the words clear and to draw you close to His heart as you read, wrote, doodled, and prayed.

If this book helped you in your relationship with Jesus, please take three action steps.

>> Check out www.3story.org—a great web site dedicated to you and your growing friendship with Jesus. You will especially like the DailyBide section. These outstanding daily readings will connect you more fully to God's Story and give you the encouragement necessary to keep moving forward. Click on God's Story on the front page of the web site to find a new entry every day, five days per week.

>> Consider reading through this book a second time with a friend who also wants to connect with Jesus. If you need another book, you can order one at www.crossway.com.

>> Take a minute *right now* to thank God! He is the one who pursues each of us and leads us on this journey every day. He wants us to live in His Story. He will give you the power to love and serve Him. Go on—try it now: Say thank you to God for helping you go deeper into His Great Love Story.

We feel proud to travel with you on this amazing adventure of following Jesus Christ. Thanks for using our book. Thanks for the attention you are giving to your relationship with God. Thanks for your courage and commitment!

⁹And it is my prayer that your love may abound more and more, with knowledge and all discernment, ¹⁰so that you may approve what is excellent, and so be pure and blameless for the day of Christ, ¹¹filled with the fruit of righteousness that comes through Jesus Christ, to the glory and praise of God. (Philippians 1:9-11)

Living the Story with you,
Your friends at Youth for Christ

Acknowledgments

We feel grateful! *Living the Story: Your Growing Relationship with Jesus* was an incredibly fun book to write!

Very special thanks go to our team of student editors who helped us keep it real. We love and appreciate you: Katelyn Columbia (Denver, Colorado), Christian Edwards (Jacksonville, Florida), Danielle Edwards (Jacksonville, Florida), Emily K. Yost (Huntington, Indiana), and Mark Wiley (Huntington, Indiana).

Lots of appreciation goes to our friends at The Livingstone Corporation. Thank you, Dave Veerman, life-long friend of YFC. You inspire us and make us look a lot smarter than we really are!

We feel honored that *Living the Story* is published by our friends at Crossway. Your commitment to serving Jesus, your love for the YFC family, and your humble dedication to God's written Word draws our hearts always closer to the Father.

The amazing privilege of standing with the great cloud of witnesses (Hebrews 12:1-2) that makes up the family of Youth for Christ is a beautiful thing. For almost seventy years of loving kids, loving God, and serving the Church, we thank YFC and count it an honor to offer this book to the Kingdom on your behalf.

For the King's Glory and His Story,
The Authors

Jenny Morgan, YFC/USA, Denver

Trent Bushnell, Lansing, MI YFC

Jack

Jack Crabtree, Long Island, NY YFC

Teddi

Teddi Pettee, Sacramento, CA YFC

Nina

Nina Edwards, YFC/USA, Denver

Tara

Tara Posen, Southern California YFC

Byron

Byron Emmert, YFC/USA, Denver

What Is 3Story®?
GOD'S STORY, MY STORY, THEIR STORY

3Story® is a way of life that guides followers of Christ to *be* good news while telling stories of *the* Good News.

Based squarely on relationships and the way we see Jesus respond to people in the Bible, 3Story focuses on a Jesus style of living.

Three overlapping circles represent three stories. The three interconnected stories reveal how relationships grow with God and with our friends. 3Story enables us to live and practice a way of life that closely resembles Jesus' way of life—connecting with God, loving the people around us, and inviting our friends into God's Story.

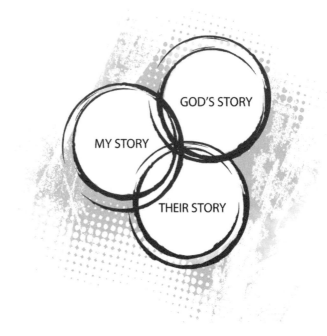

> [14]*For Christ's love compels us, because we are convinced that one died for all, and therefore all died.* [15]*And he died for all, that those who live should no longer live for themselves but for him who died for them and was raised again.* (2 Corinthians 5:14-15, NIV)

This passage shows us that what is supposed to compel us in this life is love. So love drives us in 3Story. 3Story is like love unleashed in us and through us! Being compelled by love is what 3Story is all about, therefore we learn . . .

>> to love
>> to listen
>> to be real
>> to tell stories naturally

John 15 and 1 John 4 teach us that abiding in Christ is crucial to the 3Story way of life. If followers of Christ consistently abide in Christ, 3Story will happen almost effortlessly. And the fruit of our lives will be beautiful! That's why 3Story is not a method and not a tool for ministry but rather a way of life that guides us to be something in this world while we tell stories of the Good News.

Two commandments from the Bible are at the heart and soul of 3Story.

The Great Commandment, seen in Matthew 22:34-40, says, *You shall love the Lord your God with all your heart and with all your soul and with all your mind . . . and . . . You shall love your neighbor as yourself.*

Loving God means abiding, which is really our response to His outrageous, extravagant, matchless love for us.

By ourselves we are not capable of loving the God of the universe, but with the help and guidance of the Holy Spirit we can love Him. And because God is love, loving our neighbor is an expression of our love for God.

Other passages of Scripture guide our way of life in the area of loving God and loving others: John 15:10-13; Mark 12:30-31; 1 John 4:11-12; Romans 13:9; Galatians 5:6; and James 2:8.

At the heart and soul of 3Story is the Great Commission, seen in Matthew 28:18-20. Jesus came to His disciples and said, [18]*All authority in heaven and on earth has been given to me.* [19]*Go therefore and make disciples of all nations, baptizing them in the name of the Father and of the Son and of the Holy Spirit,* [20]*teaching them to observe all that I have commanded you. And behold, I am with you always, to the end of the age.*

His presence in our lives ("I am with you always") is the first connection between My Story and God's Story. Making disciples is the connection between My Story and Their Story.

3Story is about loving relationships with God, loving relationships between people in the family of God, and loving relationships with people outside the family of

God—relationships that are loving, authentic, and meaningful. Anything that violates love violates 3Story.

3Story leads us to

>> abide in Christ every day.
>> the heart and soul of the matter—two important commandments: The Great Commandment and The Great Commission (Matthew 22:37-39 and Matthew 28:18-20).
>> love that compels us and flows through our lives.

3Story is about

>> hope more than judgment
>> stories more than steps
>> questions more than answers
>> the Holy Spirit's leading more than programs
>> listening more than telling
>> being real more than being perfect
>> love more than knowledge

The 3Story way of life emphasizes loving relationships and being real with others while understanding how storytelling affects our lives. In 3Story I learn more about My Story, how My Story ties into God's Story, and how to connect my friends' stories into God's Story.

Living the Story: Your Growing Relationship with Jesus is a companion book to the 3Story Bibles—*God's Story as Told by John* and *God's Story* (the full Bible). Thousands of Christ followers have been encouraged and liberated by this way of life. 3Story Bible resources are available from Crossway Books (www.crossway.com). 3Story training curriculum for students is available at Youth Specialties (www.youth-specialties.com). For more information about the 3Story® way of life, visit www.3Story.org.

The Ministries of Youth for Christ

CITY LIFE: YFC's City Life ministry helps young people in urban communities through teaching life skills, offering relationships with caring adults, providing opportunities for positive peer group experiences, and sharing the Good News of a relationship with Jesus Christ.

TEEN PARENTS: YFC's Teen Parents ministry connects Christian adult mentors with young women who are pregnant as well as with teenage parents. Hosting programs designed to help mothers make good choices for themselves and for their babies is only the beginning. The goal of Teen Parents is to establish young parents in a solid foundation with Jesus Christ.

YOUTH GUIDANCE: YFC's Youth Guidance ministry reaches troubled young people through juvenile justice and social service agencies. Youth Guidance connects them with trained Christian adults who help them make good choices and find healing and new life in Jesus Christ.

CAMPUS LIFE: YFC's Campus Life ministry reaches middle school and senior high young people by combining healthy relationships with creative programs, helping them make good choices, establishing a solid foundation for life, and positively impacting their schools for Christ. Campus Life is a place to make friends, talk about everyday life, and discover the beginning of a lifelong relationship with Jesus Christ.

STUDENT LED MINISTRY: YFC's Student Led Ministry inspires Christian students on high school and middle school campuses, encouraging them to live out their faith in the context of their campus community, naturally inviting others to follow Christ with them. Student Led Ministry connects YFC with local churches and other like-minded partners, using Christian adult coaches to help students become authentic, lifelong followers of Christ.

For information on the above YFC ministries in your city, go to www.yfc.net and click on USA Ministries.

YFCAMP (www.yfc.org/camp): YFC's YFCAMP exists to create an outdoor environment that invites God to transform the lives of young people through shared experiences, outdoor challenges, and times of solitude. Camps are offered in a variety of locations throughout the summer.

WORLD OUTREACH (www.yfc.org/worldoutreach): YFC/USA's World Outreach Division sends USA missionaries to serve with the indigenous ministries of YFC International in over a hundred nations worldwide. Internships are also available in numerous countries.

PROJECT SERVE® (www.projectserve.org): For three decades, YFC's Project Serve has sent thousands of young people and adults on mission trips in partnership with over ninety indigenous YFC ministries around the world.

MYM AND MCYM (www.yfc.org/mym): YFC's Military Youth Ministry equips ministry centers in the USA with resources and training to reach military youth in their community.

NATIONAL INTERNSHIPS (www.joinyfc.org): YFC's internships are focused on giving college students an opportunity to experience youth ministry. Opportunities range from working directly with teenagers to discovering what goes on behind the scenes. YFC invests in developing skills as well as helping interns clarify Jesus' call on their own life. Internships are available across the US and in many countries.

3STORY.org (www.3Story.org): 3Story® is a way of life that guides followers of Christ to *be* good news while telling stories of *the* Good News. A variety of resources and curricula are available to encourage students and adults as they live 3Story lives.

Personal Reflections

Personal Reflections

....

....

....

....

....

....

....

....

....

....

Personal Reflections

·························   ·····························

·························   ·····························

·························   ·····························

·························   ·····························

·························   ·····························

·························   ·····························

·························   ·····························

·························   ·····························

·························   ·····························

·························   ·····························

Personal Reflections

Personal Reflections

....

....

....

....

....

....

....

....

....

Personal Reflections

....

....

....

....

....

....

....

....

....

....

Personal Reflections

....

....

....

....

....

....

....

....

....

Personal Reflections

....

....

....

....

....

....

....

....

....

Personal Reflections

....

....

....

....

....

....

....

....

....

....